EMP Specific LUDDISM

STOP THE PROGRESS, I WANT TO GET OFF!

by

J. Ronald Adair

Published by

ELTEK Publishing

v1.02

Copyright ©2016 by J. Ronald Adair

All rights reserved. This book may not be reproduced in its entirety in any form, including electronic media, except by explicit, prior written permission of the publisher. Brief sections may be excerpted for review or comment.

Foreword

Although the title of this book hints at a comedic tongue-in-cheek treatment, the actual content provides concrete steps and actions to regain control of the current out-of-control human experience. The following will not be a total solution, nor a precise blueprint. Rather I hope to identify the problem, what things have contributed to it, and some principles to assist you to 'jump from the train'.

I enjoy observing, analyzing and writing about human behavior, and how those behaviors contribute to certain conditions that affect average people.

Understanding this dynamic explains why things are the way they are, and whether the massive inertia in trends and 'progress' can be controlled or managed by the average person.

I think it can, at least on a personal level. But it takes education, critical thinking, and the will and tenacity of a 'junk-yard dog'. Hopefully, after examining what follows, you'll agree.

> Lud·dite (lŭd′ĭt)
>
> n.
>
> 1. Any of a group of British workers who between 1811 and 1816 rioted and destroyed laborsaving textile machinery in the belief that such machinery would diminish employment.
> 2. **One who opposes technical or technological change.**

And, just to declare the proper disclaimers, the content of this book is intended for educational purposes only, and has not been approved by any of the following organizations; FDA, FCC, AMA, ADA, DEA, CIA, NSA, FBI, FAA, EPA, FDIC, FTC, IRS, NASA, NIH, NRLB, SEC, USPS, DHHS, DHS, CPA, MHRA, WHO, JAMA, AAA, NARP, or AARP, and wouldn't be if asked.

Introduction

Why the title of this book, you might ask? And, what's wrong with the way things are?

To explain; I believe firmly that a 20-30yr old could not meaningfully write a book on this subject. That's because their lifespan is too short. Instead, it takes someone who has lived and observed over multiple generations covering some of the most dramatic advancements in human history. It also doesn't hurt to have worked in many aspects of technology, from a starting point of pretty primitive tech to today. That's me.

So, how to explain? Did I, a techno-dweeb who was immersed for many years in the creation, manufacturing and implementing of gee-whiz technology turn on the very things that paid the bills, and kept me intellectually engaged? Or does the inherent wisdom that comes with growing older put things into different perspectives? Or perhaps I bumped into a simple-living zealot and got 'religion'? I'm not sure I can put my finger on a single action, but I do think there have been some disturbing advancements that not only make *me* uncomfortable, but a good number of others.

This book's purpose is NOT to change the world, or point out trends that should be demonstrated or legislated against. There's no appeal in this book to civil resistance and sabotage like Ned Ludd's fellow textile workers in 1811.

The purpose is to identify the trends and problems, and provide pathways for *individuals* to pursue if *they* so wish. Then, if a person really feels that they want to 'stop the progress and get off', they should be able to do so. How should society view them? Not as classic 1811 Luddites, but applying the considerations contained in this book, we could apply the term 'Selective' Luddites. I like this - Selective Luddites.

Contents

Foreword 2

Introduction 3

Chapter 1 A Short History of How We Got Here 5

Chapter 2 Modernist Life – The Up-side, The Down-side 9

Chapter 3 The Modernists' Goals 14

Chapter 4 The Modernists' Ally - Modern Marketing 21

Chapter 5 Lemming or Salmon? 25

Chapter 6 Islands of Resistance Today 27

Chapter 7 How to Get Off the 'Progress' Train 33

Chapter 8 Jumping Even Further 55

Chapter 9 Mapping Out a New Path 71

Chapter 10 Important Addendum 75

Chapter 11 Luddism Nuggets 81

Chapter 12 Real Life Luddite Examples 87

End Notes 91

From the Author 92

Chapter 1 A Short History of How We Got Here

The scene:

The time was the early 19th century, the early beginnings of the industrial revolution. Goods had been traditionally created by tradesmen, craftsmen, and artisans in a cottage industry setting. In the period between 1811-1816, new inventions brought mechanized tools that efficiently performed weaving and other textile-based jobs, threatening to seriously jeopardize these craftsmen's livelihood, their whole way of life. What to do? Why, destroy all of the automated machinery wherever it was found and preserve their means of income, of course.

There was a young man by the name of Ned Ludd, who in 1779 reportedly became the first one to do this, although it seems to be a reaction to being personally insulted by his father instead of leading a revolution. However, his action became a model, a rallying cry, and he became a phantom leader of those that followed, that really *did* do smashing and destroying. These ones became known as 'Luddites' after Ned Ludd's name, and became quite a disruptive force in merry old England, even at one time having more British soldiers fighting the Luddites than battling Napoleon.

So, in essence, the Luddites were against this particular progress (not all progress), and popular use of the term traditionally became applied to people that were against all progress – throwbacks as it were.

How does this short bit of history apply to us today? From the earliest start of the industrial revolution into the earliest stages of the technological revolution, the change was incremental, gradual, and more or less linear. Anyone making the case that new advancements were affecting jobs and professions (referred to by the term Luddite Fallacy[1]) were met by economists that believed that technological and industrial innovations created jobs and opportunities. For the greater part of the 20th century this optimistic belief held sway. But in the early 21st century studies are now showing that technological unemployment on a macroeconomic scale may indeed be increasing with technological innovation.

Why would this be happening? The answer is both simple and complex. To illustrate, consider:

> Did new and better looms create even newer and better looms? No!
>
> Did new and better trains create even newer and better trains? No!
>
> Do new and better airplanes create even newer and better airplanes? No!
>
> Do new and better computers create even newer and better computers? YES!

The computer is the game changer. Whereas most industrial and technological innovation has been done by men's minds (a constant), using normal tools (another constant), the computer and those technologies closely allied to it, has been *assisting* technologists in creating new and more powerful computers. Those improved computers then assist them in creating newer and more powerful computers, and so on.

This is the singular creation of the technological age that is outside of the historical design cycle. Most all other inventions and innovations are still advancing at a semblance of a linear progression, while computer development is advancing at an exponential rate.

Are improved computers undesirable? I remember my first computer and I don't think I want to exchange my current one for it. But, that's just a desktop personal computer – the term 'computer' is broader than this. It is now in the form of supercomputers, distributed networks, clusters, massively parallel systems -- miniaturized for use in 'smart' devices such as phones and tablets, and embedded in hundreds of appliances and machines.

However, the most significant development in computer design is artificial intelligence (AI). AI software is orders of magnitude beyond the normal computer operating system. Even though AI is just a number of years old, it is advancing rapidly and AI is being used to design newer computer technology, including the next AIs. The state of AI has prompted some warnings and concerns from a number of technology pioneers.[2]

A side-effect to this level of computing power is the ability for the computer to not only design newer and better versions of itself, but newer and better versions of every other technological product. This, in turn, modifies the near linear curve of other technology development into a near exponential one.

And this is why we are seeing a massive, increasingly fast introduction to new products, improved products, sophisticated services, and near-magic technologies.

If you look at the communications graph in the following chapter, you will see a rough representation of the technology development curve, since communications is a reflection of the technologies behind it.

So, in a nutshell, this is how we have gotten to this point. Is it bad? Some have concerns. After all, an exponential growth curve by definition has an uncertain endpoint. How fast can it continue? How advanced will it be? Will humanity lose control of the monster that they have created and can barely control now? Will our advanced technology disintegrate into a 'Mad Max' scenario, thereby finally defining where the curve ends?

To be honest, most people do not see a problem. New Tech is great, rapid change is exciting, and a sci-fi future will cure all of mankind's ills.[3]

When I watched Star Trek or other future hi-tech shows, I had a specific reality disconnect (in addition to warp drive depictions!). The reason being the technology was amazingly advanced, but it was still the same old flawed humans involved. Looking back over thousands of years of man's history, we are witness to these flaws.

Creating dangerous high technology without improved humans does not seem to be a winning plan. This is the most disturbing part of the view of the future and why there is an increasing appeal to Luddite thinking for many.

Additionally, there is another concern that I touched upon a few paragraphs back - the growth of AI. Will AI be patterned after man to the point of emulating his imperfections? Or will an AI be created *without* man's imperfections – and if so, how will that AI perceive *us*? Will an AI perceive *itself* as Man 2.0 and feel that version 1 should no longer be supported? With AI or without AI, there is still this to ponder:

"Power tends to corrupt and absolute power corrupts absolutely".
Lord Acton

Yes, as long as we have greed, a drive for fame, and lusts for power, we can imagine what the result can be when you amplify these nasty characteristics with technology able to control people's thoughts, actions, and physical environment.

First digital electronic computer,
ENIAC (Electronic Numerical Integrator And Computer) 1946

Chapter 2 Modernist Life – The Up-side, The Down-side

Up-side

No one can deny that the many advances, inventions, and comforts produced in the last 100-200yrs are of benefit. These advances encompass medical care, housing, energy, transportation and communication. And, the rapid growth of the internet and inexpensive access has allowed billions of people worldwide to share and learn from each other. To understand how communication technology has permeated societies, examine the following:

Pre-electric age – Mass communication before the electric age was via handbills, newspapers, and magazines. The reach, with the exception of a few publications, was usually community limits.

Telegraph 1800's – When the telegraph was invented, the reach was dramatically extended, along with the speed of information. However, it was a point-to-point system, so it was still dependent upon the newspapers for mass distribution.

Telephone 1876 – The telephone followed the telegraph model, with one exception. It could be patched into mass broadcast systems, thus extending its reach. At its height, the global PSTN network was worldwide with almost all people having access in varying degrees. Its infrastructure laid the groundwork for the modern Internet.

Radio 1896 – Radio was a similar model to the telephone until the 'broadcast' concept was created. It then went from a point-to-point system, to a one-to-many, the first mass information distribution system.

Television 1920's – Television followed the radio model, but added graphical value with another sense, vision. This allowed the mass distribution model to become a powerful presenter of goods and services.

Computer+Telephone 1960-1970's – The advent of the personal computer (PC), plus the global PSTN served as the early internet, although it was limited to telephone signal speeds.

Broadband Internet 1990's – This is the final stop for a worldwide mass communication system. The internet infrastructure is composed of thousands of high-speed links and routers to enable millions of access points. This network is accessed by personal computers, smartphones, tablets, and other devices. Because the speed is far above the audio limited PSTN of decade's past, it has enabled a richer variety of media, and enabled a massive transfer of the commerce model from the local general store to online purchasing and marketing.

The following graph visually illustrates the number of people reached with the various technological developments and world population:

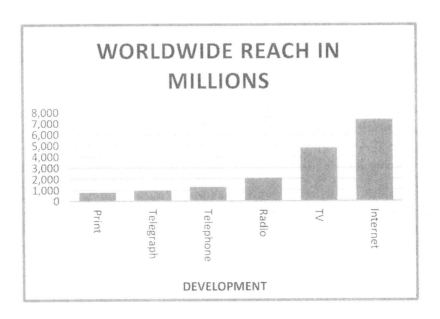

The previous analysis, although focusing on rapid communications growth, is also a reflection of other areas: transportation, product development, merchandising, government, and many more different aspects that affect all of our lives.

Down-side

As with everything, there is the inevitable Ying and Yang, pros and cons, blacks and whites, or whatever one may call it. Some refer to this cosmic balance as Karma, others may say 'unintended consequences'. The bottom line is that all of the upsides of modernist advances have fallout or side-effects. What are these? Let's examine each of them:

- Loss of privacy – 100 years ago, the issue of privacy would be a laughable concern. The issue then was the opposite – getting to know your neighbors, local businesses, and being able to be located by strangers. Compare that to today: your personal vital statistics registered with hundreds, if not thousands of marketers, businesses, governmental entities, law enforcement groups, and even criminals. In addition, your financial information is on file with countless commercial institutions, and the 'security' you have in place is easily cracked by determined criminals anywhere on the globe. Totalitarian-bent governments, in the interests of 'national security', will have all of this information plus access to government databases you reside in. Search and social media conglomerates have much of your personal data, plus your shopping and purchasing records - which trails you like a flock of starving chickens. If you are in any country that isn't total third world, then much of your personal information is on file. Some people don't like this.
- Mental overload – Modern life requires a lot of mental activity. Here are some samples: account numbers, deposits, licenses, fees, taxes, logon IDs, passwords, inspections, insurance, mortgages, phone numbers, medical appointments and records, dietary requirements,

prescription drug tracking, child vaccinations, school events, relative and friend's birthdays and anniversaries, etc. etc. Compare this to life in 'Little House on the Prairie' and you get an idea how the mental overload has grown and shows no sign of slowing down.

- Unnecessary expense – Because of the powerful marketing forces surrounding us today, we are enticed, cajoled, and herded into spending money for goods and services. Some of these are for legitimate *needs*, but much of it is for *wants*. Determining the difference between needs and wants takes mature thinking ability and values. That is why much of the marketing efforts are targeted to the young and lesser educated. With the availability of easy credit, one does not have to even have the funds on-hand to obtain immediate *wants* – credit is available. Hence the cycle is: entice, sell, borrow, buy and pay. The merchandisers depend on these steps as an ongoing state.
- Skewed values – The amusing grave marker engraving, 'He who dies with the most toys wins', demonstrates the end result of the hyped marketing of 'wants' in the modern economy. This is, of course, meant to be a tongue-in-cheek statement, but unfortunately, this attitude permeates much of today's demographics. Possessions equal 'success'. Gadgets and toys demonstrate human 'value', and 'Lifestyles of the Rich and Famous' becomes obsessive for those that are neither rich or famous. But add a credit-line and for a short while you can *seem* like you're rich. That is, until the collector comes calling and then it is servitude to the credit and banking industry - or bankruptcy. The laudable values of decades and centuries past are no longer present, replaced by a party atmosphere with the revelers enslaved to others that don't really care about them.
- High stress – A companion to the previous points is a large load of stress. This stress is most present to those that have some ethical belief that they should obey the rules, pay the bills, and do the things that those in higher authority tell them to do. Statistics show that the stress load for individuals has increased greatly in later decades because of

obligations and economic pressures.[4] Add to the personal stress the stress caused by world conditions, which, not surprisingly, is brought into our lives by the same communication infrastructure that brings us immersive commercial marketing.

Chapter 3 The Modernists' Goals

The truth is that the vast majority of people tend to a modernist view, i.e. progress, new things, gee-whiz toys, etc. So, alongside the market forces and consumer manipulation, there is a strong drive for individuals to facilitate this rush. Therefore, to help all of us Selective Luddites understand where it is heading, here is a list of some of the stated goals the 'modernists' are striving for.

Food - 'A chicken in every pot'

This phrase, from FDR in 1944 was a campaign slogan. It indicated that no one was going to be hungry, and because he didn't say 'beans and rice' in every pot, it showed that it would not be just subsistence. Since a chicken represented a food that ALL classes enjoyed, it was a great equalizer, so that we would all be equal and all be well-fed!

Today's idealists see this as a foundation – if hunger is eliminated, then it allows for everyone to unleash his potential. How is this to be accomplished? By the following:

- Large, highly mechanized factory farms with standardized methodology, genetically enhanced crops, artificial fertilizers that can be mass produced for increasing yields, robotic systems to eliminate undependable human workers, and mono-crop specialization for efficiency.
- Mass-produced factory food that is inexpensive and that can alleviate *hunger*.

While the stated goals are certainly laudable, the means of obtaining them are problematic. What are some concerns?

- o The compromising of food quality and proper nourishment.
- o The promotion of mono-culture, or crops that are the easiest to cultivate, harvest, and distribute.
- o Standardization of varieties controlled by GMO based global corporations.

- o Restriction of individual choice by a state-controlled food system managed by bureaucrats and influenced by corporate lobbyists.

How about housing?

Utopian visions for housing in the past was the 'hive' concept. This vision was implemented with cookie-cutter housing units in high rise buildings (height is a more efficient utilization of land), and an urban environment. This has changed somewhat, but the goal of 'cookie-cutter' state-controlled housing is still present. This vision works best in urban settings, which promotes ever larger cities with high density housing.

Transportation

Mass transportation (again, government controlled) is the modernists' preferred choice over individual gas-powered vehicles unless driverless and automated.5 The key element is efficiency and the belief of declining natural resources. Although currently, air transportation is not as efficient as ground, modernists embrace air travel because in a gee-whiz world, air travel is a must.
One of the problems with government-controlled high technology mass travel systems is the loss of privacy. This is because of the billing and security systems required for these type systems. Compare this to a man on horseback or bicycle.

Work

Man's 'work' description has changed from hunter, gatherer, warrior, to include farmer, trader, artisan, then adding factory worker, clerical, serviceman, and finally creator, scientist, technologist.
During all of this time, people farmed, sold their services via small businesses, and worked for others. The one working for others had a 'job'. The majority of people in developed countries in the 19th and 20th centuries worked at 'jobs'.

The major cost component of almost all goods and services is the labor cost. In addition to the salaries paid, there is an additional cost of employment referred to as the 'burden'. This is made up of the insurance, social programs contribution, unemployment and accident and sickness taxes. So, businesses and business management must contain this cost and if possible, *reduce* it to stay competitive in the market.

The major labor efficiency improvement action taken has been better tools and more advanced processes. The logical next step was robotic manufacturing. As the cost of robotic technology goes down (which it is), and the sophistication of robotics goes up (which it is), then most manual labor, and many service 'jobs' become overtaken by robots.[6] As robotics becomes more advanced, the rest of the service-based jobs - teaching, medical, and scientific - all become obsolete. What will humans do? Why, recreation, artistic activities (although robots may do it better), and games (just don't play a robot). All of this non-productive fun will be paid for with taxes from robotic activities to be redistributed to the populace (by government).

Quality of Life

Obviously the modernist vision of recreation and life quality can expand now that AI's and robots do all the work. People can manage moods with designer drugs and immersive virtual reality role-playing, won't go hungry because robot-managed factory farms and manufactured nutrition will be present for everyone, and will be healthier because of genetic control of not only humans, but viruses, bacteria, disease-carrying insects, and plants and animals. Because of advanced genetic management, parents can have designer offspring and anyone can have undesirable features modified so that they can be smart *and* beautiful!

Before all the millennials reading become ecstatic with this vision, there's still just one...

Oops!

Well, ok, there's always a fly in the punchbowl. At this point, people still get old and die – and it's just *not* fair!

Sure, there are some great advancements in increasing human lifespan, and even increasing 'health-span', the science of helping us to all be healthier longer. But, that's not good enough for young modernists who believe that they have so much more art and music left to give to humanity!

No, there has to be a better way – and there is! The singularity![7] Although the singularity's main definition is of computer-caused runaway technological growth, a companion belief is of that future time where man's consciousness can be merged with a machine (preferably a sexy, sophisticated robot body). This does away with our still beautiful, active minds enslaved to a flawed and dying human body.

The singularity is the holy grail of modernists – be prepared to hear more and more about it!

Bottom Line

Of course, all of this is a lot of changes to society and many people will not get aboard. That is why it will take – guess who? Government! Yes, government(s) will have to *mandate* society to sign up. So, for potential Selective Luddites, this ups the difficulty level. However, don't despair, I firmly believe in the creative genius of most people to work around obstacles as long as the will is there! This is called 'human nature', something the modernist thinkers never consider.

In 1931, an English writer by the name of Aldus Huxley penned the classic novel, 'A Brave New World'. While it is beyond the scope of this book to include excerpts from Huxley's work, it needs to be required reading for all you potential Selective Luddites. Modernists have already read it and have faith that in their lifetime, *despite* human nature, it will be *different* in actual practice.

Chapter 4 The Modernists' Ally - Modern Marketing

There can be no general acceptance of modernists' goals and visions without marketing! This is because many people subconsciously feel that the rapid progress they see is a fearful path. Is there a devious master marketing plan that is driving society forward to the brave new world? No! It is, rather, a conflux of different forces that in *themselves* is not evil or detrimental. Let us examine these in turn.

Vested self-interest

All biological life has vested self-interest. If we look at the simplest lifeforms, we see that these interests are in themselves simple: eat, avoid being eaten, and reproduce. While these basic interests propagate upwards to higher order life, other more complex interests come into play. When we make our way to the highest lifeform, man (or so I've been told), we now wind up with a host of self-interests that can be just as strong motivators as avoiding being eaten. Here're some, although not a complete list:

- Praise and rewards
- Condemnation and punishment
- Pride
- Need for control
- Leadership drive
- Greed
- Materialism
- Revenge
- Validation
- Pack comfort
- Intellectual understanding

We see that for a number of these, unbalanced individuals will give up, or greatly diminish, the basic interests that are present in us all. A good example would be a monk foregoing marriage and family for praise, rewards, and pack comfort. Another would be a scientist so engrossed in intellectual pursuits that he forgets to eat. Or, celebrities that sacrifice normal personal relationships in the quest for 'fame'.

So, since marketing experts understand these drives and interests, they will formulate campaigns to appeal to them, AND they are also driven by the same interests! The marketing mind doesn't have to be a sinister plot; it is what it is.

Creative instinct

The creative instinct is a part of the human makeup. However, it is stronger in some people than others. For the creative person, there is never a drive to un-create, or un-invent. Rather, it is always a drive to improve, discover new ways, create breakthroughs. Once you understand this aspect of human behavior, you will understand why the march of development and 'progress' is running pedal-to-the-metal.

Group-think

Group dynamics should not be overlooked in modernist advancement. The advantages of small groups (not large ones) in the innovation and development activities are several: instant feedback from members, stair-stepping ideas, testing of new directions, and dampening of runaway quests. Even though many great developments in the past have been brought to birth by lone creators, the small group is driving the fast-paced innovation today.

Saturation Sales Pitches

If the marketing level was at the level of the 1930-1950s, there wouldn't be much of an issue - however, it isn't. What level is it today? Let us count the ways:

- Newspaper – yes, it is still present from its start in the 1800s.
- Magazines – most magazines are vehicles for advertisements, sometimes, there is content included.
- Radio – started in the 1900s and still going strong, just more and more cleverly packaged.

- TV – started in the 1950s and like radio, is pervasive and so masterfully packaged that certain prime-time commercials will convince you to ask your doctor for a drug that has a stated list of side-effects that could eliminate the population of a medium sized country.
- Internet – the newest and most saturated medium yet for marketing. There are now web pages that have so many ad pitches that they have become essentially non-functional. Search engines, blog platforms, news pages, email services, etc. etc. etc. The Internet is marketing's most holy in the temple of mass sales.

Add to the above: marketing on sports venues and players, NASCAR vehicles, public transit vehicles, smart device 'apps', and even government-owned buildings, and we see that whatever the commercial world has developed and is selling, there is the ever-present marketing machine to make sure that products and services are 'consumed' by the consumer, whether it is a *need* or not![8]

The term 'consumer' has a powerful position in the modernist world. Economists use it to define economic models, governments use it to grade the health of their economies, and businesses create whole strategies targeting the 'consumer'.

You are a consumer if you purchase and use anything produced by others. The challenge is, just like food, to consume only what is needed to be healthy, and not be a glutton or be force-fed.

Chapter 5 Lemming or Salmon?

Let's imagine a scene. You are in a swift-flowing river, bumping along near the bank, bouncing off rocks – you desperately grasp at grass and limbs on the bank to slow your motion. In the middle of the stream are rubber tubes and floats filled with young generationals, laughing and paddling furiously to see who can take the lead. Glancing into the water, you can spot large Salmon swimming against the flow. Being a wiser person, your reasoning and experience tells you that with this much water flow, there has to be a precipitous drop somewhere downstream. You can just imagine you hear a faint roar, but you cannot be sure. However, that observation urges you to *not* float downstream, but like the Salmon, swim upstream to a different goal.

Imaginary, yes. But with the powerful marketing and manipulative forces employed by commerce and ruling organizations, it is no wonder that the great majority of human beings are swept along in the streams of 'progress' in an uncontrolled manner. These streams are so prevalent, that it takes educated individuals with strong critical thinking abilities and the tenaciousness of junk-yard dogs to swim in an opposite direction.

Another scenario is the Lemming tale. The pull of peer pressures, manufactured desires, and your own weaknesses will herd you into a vast Lemming rush to an unknown end.

A good example is the smartphone demands by children. While many parents believe that getting a smartphone into their children's hands at an early age is a great thing, others may not. However, it really doesn't *matter* what they believe, as the pressure upon their children by their peers and the saturated marketing to young people will *make* this happen. If parents don't give into their children's demands, then they will be perceived as cruel, uncaring, and uncool. What is the easiest thing to do? Why give in, of course. It matters not whether the smartphone is detrimental to a young person's emotional and intellectual development (these points are even now being extensively documented - see Chapter 10), it is the path of *least resistance*.

Another example is the automobile game. Marketing does its best to convince 'consumers' that your 3-year old clunker HAS to be traded in TODAY! Just come on down to Earl's and you will get 'top' dollar for your trade-in, no money down and an easy 480-month loan at giveaway rates. Why, you might even qualify for a what? – FACTORY REBATE! Yep, easy as getting into that obsolete car of yours and turning the key!

And, we can't leave out the fast food industry, can we? Years ago, people gathered produce from their gardens or bought ingredients from their local markets, and prepared meals in their own kitchens. They did this because they got hungry, but also to fuel their bodies so they could perform work.

Today, we have saturation advertising urging us to buy *recreation* food. Food that makes you feel like part of the group, be young and beautiful, funny and cool. No information is presented that states that this particular food product will keep you healthy, enhance your immune system, slow down aging, or provide boundless energy. No, the message is an appeal to a whole range of positive human emotions – none that have to do with nutrition!

You can be a lemming and go with the flow while not making waves, or you can be the Salmon that swims against the current.

Becoming a Selective Luddite will create in you a Salmon personality. You may not be able to fully swim upstream, but you may make enough lifestyle changes to at least swim in place – either action is good.

Chapter 6 Islands of Resistance Today

If you are convinced that resistance is futile, then take heart! There are groups of people even today that are practicing Selective Luddism, whether they know it as that or not. Let's examine some of the ones we know of. The reason I state 'know of' is that some individuals are so successful in dropping off-grid, that we don't even know about them. Hats off, I say! Here are some we DO know of:

Religious-

There have been a number of religious groups throughout history that have practiced isolation. This is because of a belief that mixing with ones not of their faith could compromise their beliefs and moral standards. Here are a couple today that are well-known.

Amish

The most familiar religious group that maintains isolation from the modern world is the Amish. The Amish are known for simple living, plain dress, and reluctance to adopt many conveniences of modern technology. They value rural life, manual labor and humility, all under the auspices of living what they interpret to be God's word.

Old Order Mennonites

While some of the reformed and modern Mennonites are plugged in to the modern lifestyle, some branches, just like the Amish, still try to isolate themselves in enclaves and ward off outside influences.

Non-religious –

It doesn't necessarily take religious teachings for many to recognize dangers from mixing with outsiders.

And, in many cases, it is justified. We can agree that if the native Hawaiian Island inhabitants could have had a choice when European explorers came calling, they would have taken it (since they didn't have smallpox inoculations yet). Here are some non-religious groups:

Isolated Tribes

There are a number of isolated tribes of people that have been discovered. These are islands of self-sufficient societies that in many cases know nothing of the 'modern' world, and will have nothing to do with it. The reasons for their isolation vary – from religious beliefs to having a workable community with a system of justice and peaceful existence. Here are just a few as a sampling:

- Sentinelese – These are an indigenous people of the Andaman Islands, in the Bay of Bengal. They are a hunter-gatherer society with an unclassified language and a tendency to kill visitors.
- Korowai – A tree-house dwelling people living in Papua, New Guinea. They didn't know of outside people until possibly 1970. They do have a specific language – Korowai.
- The Mashco-Piro Tribe – This is what is left of an Amazon tribe nearly exterminated by the army of Carlos Fitzcarrald. They are hard to find, and understandably don't want to have anything to do with outsiders.
- The Pintupi Aboriginals – The Pintupi lived in the Western Desert of Australia, one of the last aboriginal groups to leave their traditional lifestyle - mainly because of some 1960s missile tests that tended to impact in their homeland.

Off-grid

Off-grid participants have a number of different motivations: cost of living savings, the desire to be left alone and not be a number in a machine, some survivalist leanings, and anger at infrastructure systems because of abuses and injustices.

Survivalists

The movie 'Tremors' had the best depiction of a survivalist couple with Reba McIntyre and Michael Gross playing Burt and Heather Gummer. The Gummers lived in a hilltop fortress with a basement full of armaments that could equip a third world army.

While this was a humorous view of a survivalist, survivalists today are mostly equipping themselves to be self-sufficient in the event of catastrophic infrastructure failures, food and water shortages, electrical grid breakdowns, and biologic pandemics.

Minimalists

- Minimalists differ from others because of the reasons that motivate them. The minimalist selects a lifestyle to reduce mental stress and gain life quality. Unless you set your heart on becoming a member of the Sentinelese Tribe, this may be one of the better avenues for practicing Selective Luddism.
- Minimalists selectively embrace and reject the things surrounding them with the goal of improving the quality of their lives.
- They have come to a realization that the quality of their lives does not depend upon an abundance of 'things' or activities.
- They do not practice minimalism in preparation, like survivalists, for a coming Apocalypse, but more as a lifestyle change for better quality of life.
- Selective Luddism is closest in practice to minimalism.

Rugged Individualists

There are a number of different lifestyles in this category, with varying degrees of separation from the modernist world. Let's examine just a few:

- Cowboys - The American cowboy history has always been one of individualism, making do with just the necessities of life, and living and working in an outdoor environment. Much of this cowboy lifestyle can be seen today with a few exceptions; the business aspects have become high-tech and modernist, there is more use of modern materials, and even though today's cowboy can still sit on a hand-tooled saddle on a well-trained horse, it is not unusual to spot a cellphone in his hand.
- Trappers – In the old American west, the 'trapper' was the epitome of a rugged individualist. A trapper would make a

trip to the general store and stock up on basic supplies that could support him for weeks in the wilderness. He would then traverse wilderness areas, many times during harsh winter conditions, setting traps over many miles of territory. He would have a wilderness cabin or shelter and would live off his meager supplies and what he could trap or kill for food. This was a hard life, but it appealed to many that could live without close human contact, and knew how to provide for themselves. There are a few of these mindsets today although they may not be actually trapping and selling furs.

- Explorers – The explorer class are those ones that have an intense interest in places, things, history or people (sometimes). They own very little 'stuff', usually have no stationary home, and are mobile. This constant movement prevents them from gathering the trappings of modern life.
- Warriors – Warriors are similar to explorers, except are comfortable in more disciplined structures. Some of these are the military, soldiers of fortune, troubleshooters, and certain dangerous jobs that set them apart from the average person.
- The RV set – Many couples, upon reaching retirement, sell their paid-for home and their furnishings and personal effects, have multiple garage sales for all the rest of their accumulated 'junk', and invest their funds in a recreational vehicle. They then rent spaces in RV parks around the country, moving with the changing weather. They have RV friends and peers, and lead a minimalist lifestyle with greatly reduced stress.

Functional Anarchists

Anarchists are in the list by virtue of their stated goals; i.e. the destruction of governments, ruling classes, and systems. However, anarchists today are somewhat puzzling in that they arrive at anarchist activities via highly developed and precisely operating air travel systems, use high-tech social media to organize and plan, and contact other anarchists with the latest smartphones. It would seem this isn't fully isolating oneself from modernist society, but what do I know?

Street people

To complete this topic, there is a relatively new group that fits into this role – most, sadly, not by choice. There have always been street people going back to the earliest cities and urban centers, but there has been a change the last 40-50 years. In many areas, street people have been assisted by political groups to receive the 'necessities of life'. These necessities include food and water, shelter, and a voice in the management of their affairs.

There are 'homeless' settlements in many large cities. While most of the homeless would welcome having jobs, homes, and a 'normal' life, there are some that embrace this lifestyle. These are people that can't mentally or emotionally handle the complexities of modern life (potential Selective Luddites?). They do not have the ability to handle the worry about paying bills, taxes, insurance, commuting, workplace stresses, marketing urgings and similar other 'normal' activities. Some of these concerns would be great goals for anyone – but becoming homeless is not the road to take!

Chapter 7 How to Get Off the 'Progress' Train

So, what can we learn from these groups and individuals? First, that even though difficult, it is not impossible to become a Selective Luddite.

The goals we want to pursue are; avoiding the trappings of modernism that negatively impact the quality of our life, while adopting the things that are beneficial or necessary. So a selection process must be exercised, one that is honest, balanced and attainable. While joining the Mashco-Piro Tribe might be doable, it would not be easy, and probably not a good goal.

And, that's what Selective Luddism is for, making the choices that make sense. Here are some points to consider:

- What can I do to resist the extreme marketing forces thrown my way, especially toward all family members?
- What can I do to highly reduce the paperwork I have to attend to?
- What can I do to free up more time for myself and/or family?
- What can I do to improve my diet, control my weight, and have more energy and better health?
- How can I avoid the medical treadmill?
- What can I do to reduce the amount of money required to support myself and my family?
- What can I(we) do to reduce the on-going, accumulating stress load?

> At this point in your reading of this book, you will have to make some tough decisions. If you are excited about the modernist lifestyle, look forward to the newest tech, are not fazed by crowds, traffic, high-pressure workplaces or paperwork, and actually yearn to participate in the singularity, then you probably need to just skip the rest of this book, close the cover, and we all agree to part friends (sorry, no refunds, though).
>
> If, however, you are overwhelmed and stressed out over your current lifestyle and feel the quality of your and/or your family's life is suffering, stay here. If you dread getting up to join the one hour or more commute to a job at a company that is occupied by corporate psychopaths who will sacrifice you at the drop of a paper clip, then keep reading. If you feel your health is being compromised by the modernist lifestyle and your place in it, then continue. If your financial life is desperate or you're living payday-to-payday, read on. Nobody can fix these conditions except you – no government, business, or charitable organization – just you! But, you don't have to attempt it alone. You have a powerful tool with Selective Luddism!

Testing where you are now

You can determine the state of your non-luddite life now by answering the following questions. This test will not be graded; it is just a mental exercise to see how much you are wrapped up in the modernist environment.

- How many purchases that you make are for actual *needs*, vs the purchases of *wants*? Do you know the difference?
- Can you estimate how many marketing ads you see each day? Do you think you could?
- How many social media accounts do you have? How much time do you spend with your social media community? Is it more than with your family?
- How many email accounts do you have? How much time do you spend answering and sorting emails?
- How many vehicles that require licensing, inspection and maintenance do you own?

- How many extracurricular school activities are you involved in?
- How many 'smart' devices do your family own?
- Do you use a daily planner to organize your day?
- How resistant are you to 'clickbait'?
- How long do you think you could comfortably be without your cellphone, tablet, or anything Internet?
- Do you earn all or part of your income online?
- Do you still use paper checks?
- How often do you read a *paper* book?
- How often is a made-from-scratch meal prepared in your home?
- Is the size of your walk-in closet(s) larger than many average living rooms?
- How many subscriptions (newspapers, magazines, book clubs, online services) do you have?

This is not a complete list, but hopefully enough so that you can see where the problems may lie.

Family issues

The makeup of your family determines if and how you can jump from the train. The following scenarios illustrate what I mean.

Your family is just you –

> This is pretty much a no-brainer. You have total freedom to craft an exit plan. If you are young you will make different choices than if you are older, say retirement age. The easiest scenario is if you are approaching retirement or just starting it. If you are a young person and you are making a choice to be a Selective Luddite, then you are a wise person indeed.

Your family consists of you and a partner –

> This model is very doable if both of you are of a similar mind. If you want to exit and your partner is totally immersed in the modernist lifestyle, then your choices will be limited. It doesn't mean you, individually, cannot make

selective choices to better your quality of life (QOL). In time, your partner may see the advantages you have gained, and gradually adopt some Selective Luddite actions also.

Your family consists of you, a partner, and one child –

This combo depends greatly upon the age of the child. Most children today are immersed in modernist society by the age of 6 or so, although that age is getting younger quickly. Obviously, infants and very young children would not be a problem, and by the time they become aware of a modernist world, if they are taught well, they will see their QOL is better than their peers. This holds for some of the religious isolationists, although a few do leave that lifestyle for the bright lights of the city! If the child is in the age range between infant to pre-teen, then this will be more of a challenge. Here, the partners must be able to present the alternate way in a manner to make it more appealing than the modernist world. However, since children are protected from the many negatives of modernism, they have no wisdom to be able to examine the pros and cons I covered in chapter 2. You will have the most work prying the 'smart' gadgets from their clenched little fists!

If your single child is a teenager, then it will be difficult to get them to hold your hand while you jump from the train. Teenagers are our Generation Z, and this generation has been saturated by the techno-marketing forces that we have already discussed. The glitter, gee-whiz gadgets, instant peer communication, and the Gen Z community has them in its grip. In this case, parental dictates will not work. The only reasonable choice you have is by example and patient education. Your teenager will eventually grow older and may experience (probably will) the modernist pressures that you are feeling. Remembering your example, they may also jump from the train. This scenario also applies if your family is just you and a child, but it may be more difficult.

Your family consists of you, a partner and multiple children –

This choice is similar to the above, but obviously more difficult unless all of the children are very young. If they are all teens, then good luck – save *yourself!* On the other hand, being that you will practice 'Selective' Luddism, it IS possible to remove or reduce certain aspects of modernism that cause the most angst in your life, even with resistant children.

As we see from the above, because of the variety in your family, there is no standard formula to follow.

Making the Jump

For the purpose of outlining the steps to embracing Selective Luddism, I am using the simpler model of just yourself. For an extended family, you will have to make adjustments according to the previous section.

While it is reasonable to attack the modernist area that is causing you the most pain first, it may also be the hardest to conquer. Others that may not be high on your list could be corrected simply. Since all areas contribute to your overall mental overload and stress, reducing a simple one may be the first task. It can also give you confidence that you can manage your life and see that Selective Luddism works.

I am going to take this in the order of the modernist 'cons' from chapter 2.

Privacy Loss –

Up until the 1990's privacy loss was limited to thieves digging through your trash looking for bank account numbers, business insiders marketing your personal information, and stolen credit cards, etc. But all good things end - the Internet became a part of our lives. Now, through the miracle of global technology, a Nigerian benefactor, using a cobbled-up personal computer and dialing into a local ISP, could, with a modicum of skill, browse the folders on your computer, plant key loggers so they can capture your online user ID's and passwords, and add some cool ransomware encryption for your files. All this marvelous activity can happen once you make that connection from your PC or smart device to the Internet.

So, has your 'privacy' been compromised?

Most worldly-wise folks know the things to do to protect privacy at the physical level: use shredders for your sensitive paperwork before it goes into the trash, use a lockable, slotted mailbox, no vanity tags with your name present, and other sensible actions.

However, once you connect to the Internet, buy and sell, pay bills, and check your bank account, the idea of privacy becomes quaint. Add to that the wholesale urge to post on a social media site everything about you, your family, your pets, your home repairs, your favorite restaurants (with pics), and all of your vacation plans or the vacations themselves, and we see that you not only have given up privacy, you have provided a dossier on your whole life for anyone to use and peruse. What are you thinking?!!

It is true that many of the above Internet activities are time-saving, convenient, and economical. So, to be a Selective Luddite, you just need to use what makes sense, and delete or greatly tighten your exposure on the others. Here are some things to consider to keep the advantageous but change the things that diminish your privacy. Understand that much of the focus is on *security*. **Without security, you cannot have privacy**.

Privacy Exposure	Action
Basic computer usage	While it is generally recognized that the personal computer is subjected to the most hacking attempts, it is also true that there are more counter-offensive tools available. Tablets and smartphones have become targeted more and there is a smaller inventory of counter hacking tools. For all computing platforms, here're some basic actions you can do: • Install and use a quality Anti-virus/firewall app. Read the reviews to see what the best is for you – do NOT use a

	'free' or shareware virus tool. If you have to pay a nominal fee, pay it! • Use a password utility (see next section) that stores your website URLs, user ids, and passwords in encrypted format with access via a master password. Make your master password strong and don't lose track of it.
Banking online	Assuming your computer or tablet is secure with no keystroke logging Trojans installed, online banking can be relatively secure and private. Many financial institutions employ two-factor validation. This means you enter your user ID and password, and then another action is employed to verify it is really you. A popular choice is a text sent to your cellphone, which is on file with the bank. If you are concerned about your banking being private, then opt for the two-factor validation. Banks also allow you to opt for paperless statements – for best privacy choose this so you don't leave banking records in the trash inadvertently. When logging onto your bank's website examine the URL that it really *is* your bank.
Shopping online	The more places you shop online, the more exposure you have to privacy compromises, so you may want to limit them to just a few and thoroughly vet their payment portal and security. Many online merchandisers store your payment information on their servers, and this where some digital thievery has taken place in the past. However, companies have been improving their security, so it is a pretty low risk now. Still, you usually have the option, if you're worried, to opt out of the storage of your payment information.
Social Media	The use and addiction to 'social media' is one of the worst privacy hemorrhages in history. As was mentioned elsewhere, when users go to their social media accounts, they lose their mind when it comes to privacy, posting names, ages, family info, location, schools history, work info, and many, many photos. This can become a mother-lode for identity thieves and can, in certain cases, put you or your family members at risk. Here are some things to practice when it comes to ANY 'social media' site:

	• Don't record your full name. • Same with your address and telephone numbers. • Don't use dates with school history. • Never list your parent's names and locations. • Never post your SSN or driver's license number. • Don't add ages to your children's photos. • Don't add a running visual commentary on a night out on the town! These are just some basic precautions. Of course, you may heavily use social media and never have a problem – but if you do, it could be serious. As a Selective Luddite, the *much better* choice is trash all social media sites - they are the crown jewels of the modernist lifestyle.
Bill Paying	Probably most people with computers in any form pay at least one bill online. There is no doubt that compared to the old paper way, it is a huge time saver and is much more flexible. The security issues are not much different than online purchasing, i.e., the storing of your payment information on the vendor's data center servers. This is no different than the paper method. There is not much of a privacy issue since most people that you make payments to already have much of your personal and financial information. However, there are some bill payment applications and services that can greatly free up some of your precious time.
General web surfing	Normal recreational 'surfing' of the web is one of the greatest security and privacy threats, so use a lot of caution when doing so. The following precautions should be followed: • Just because a link or graphic is clickable, doesn't *mean* you should click it to see what it does. • 'Click bait' are stories or items that appear alongside a web page that you may have explicitly browsed to. Their goal is to have you be enticed into clicking on them by presenting something really, really

	interesting (sometimes it is true). Once you are on their pages and under their marketing control, then there will be many ads presented (this is how they make money). Resist this with as much strength as you can as this is maximum marketing and against your Selective Luddism goals. • Do NOT respond to any popup 'notice' that some component of your computer needs upgrading – 'click here to do it now'. This is not true and is where much undesirable 'junkware' gets installed. • Remember, what do you NOT enter online just because someone you don't know asks you to? Your full name, address, telephone number, driver's license number, social security number, account numbers including any banking info, and any family members' information. • Porn and sexually titillating sites have more of a tendency to load up your computers with malware and other undesirable 'features'. And, you do realize that registering your credit card with these type sites is not going to be too private, right?
'Cloud' storage	There is no such thing as a physical 'cloud' connected to the internet. Cloud storage merely means that you are storing some of your information that would normally be on your personal device to storage on a server at someone's data center. There are many advantages to this: gaining additional storage over what you have on your devices, backup of data in case of accidents at your location or a lost device, and availability of your information across any of your devices. Privacy with cloud storage is a relative issue, you probably won't be having humans examining your information unless the NSA/CIA/FBI has reason to (they don't, do they?) However, having your information 'mined' by the cloud storage hosts (especially if it is free) for economic trends and marketing info is a *distinct* possibility.

These are just some of the various ways you can improve your privacy without being draconian. It is not everything that can be done, but is the most obvious steps requiring minimum effort. By selecting the modernist features that gain you time and reduce your stress load, while not greatly compromising your privacy, you are practicing Selective Luddism in a balanced and reasonable way.

Mental Overload –

How many passwords do you have to keep track of? How many vehicle inspections, tags, and registrations do you need to remember? The concept of multi-tasking, which computers can do well, humans don't. Multi-tasking behavior is driven by tackling things that have to be done in the same time-frame. The solution is to either reduce the number of things or find an improved way to manage them, including timing and scheduling. Many people, because of the number of accounts and portals that require logons, use the same password for all as it is easier to remember. THIS IS A BAD IDEA. If you use the same password that you use for your bank account and other *high security* sites as those with *minimum security*, and a hacker easily breaks the low security sites, he will use that password for your other sites. And voila! Here're some suggestions to use instead:

- Password storage applications, like LastPass, RoboForm, Dashlane, and other tools, store website URLs, user IDs, and passwords in encrypted local storage. These will be protected by a master password. You also can have the apps create complex passwords for each site, removing the commonality risk.
- Use a core password that is easy to remember, and then modify it with information from each website. For instance, you might use 'Froggy' as your base (always capitalized), and for your Bank of America account use a 'ba' prefix and the last two digits of your birth year. Since some logons require a special character, you could add a dash and your final, pretty strong (and unique) password winds up as 'ba-Froggy67'. This formula is really easy to remember but you

can use any such technique – just make it consistent so you don't forget.

Mental overload can be intense when you have an inordinate amount of obligations. These can be financial, medical, school activities, repairs, or voluntary duties that make more than reasonable demands on your time. Some of these are covered in the following *High Stress* section, but in general you must do a number of things: evaluate the amount of time you spend on obligations, decide what you can do, and make the changes that work. To do this you must be resolute in your decisions, and not let others shame you or intimidate you into doing *their* wishes, not yours.

As an example: let's assume you have accumulated over time a large number of credit cards. You have good credit and it gives you a warm sense of accomplishment when you flip open your wallet and can see all these little plastic soldiers lined up. However, to keep your good credit, you will need to pay all of these accounts on time. If you pay from the paper statement, this can be a time consuming task – if you pay online, it is somewhat better, but you will need to make sure you have all of the accounts recorded and easy to tick off so none are overlooked. Solution? Keep one or two of the higher limit and better cards, transfer the other balances to these and close the other accounts. Another solution is to only keep one credit card account for emergencies, and use bank debit cards for your daily expenses. This simple step can reduce a good amount of mental overload.

Many people get roped into obligations because they cannot say 'no'. While this may seem uncaring and cruel to not join a friend's favorite cause, you must remember that you are attempting to reduce *your* mental overload on your way to becoming a Selective Luddite. Just creatively and nicely say no!

Unnecessary Expenses –

The problem with the modernist life economically is the blurring of the lines between *needs* and *wants*. The way to take control of your expenses is to honestly identify which is which. Let us list some *basic* needs:

- Food and Drink
- Shelter
- Clothing
- Personal environment control (heating/cooling)
- Transportation
- Communication
- Recreation

We can see that *wants* can be enhancements or embellishments to *needs*, but can also be completely new categories. First, let's look at the *needs* enhancements:

- Food and Drink – Enhancement of this basic need can add unnecessary expenses to your food budget. What can these be?
    - Pre-packaged foods to save preparation time
    - Exotic fruits and vegetables (ok, if health enhancer)
    - 'Imported' waters
    - Buying name brands instead of generic
- Shelter – Sure, we all want a roof over our heads, but how much roof? Like all consumer goods, a home is marketed appealing to the same human senses and personality weaknesses. So, you need to ask yourself:
    - Is my/our home for shelter and comfort, or for show?
    - Is my home too large, making it a chore to maintain?
    - Will the size of my home require a large investment in furnishings, with the requisite care required?
    - What about the supporting costs for a large home – utilities, taxes, insurance premiums, repairs?
- Clothing – While much of your family's clothing needs can be satisfied by chain department stores, marketing pressures will attempt to move you to shop at only 'certain' stores, or 'certain' brands. This is not unusual as brand and company loyalty is a huge part of modern marketing. The advantages, of course, belong not to you but to the companies. Intelligent clothing purchasing is to pick and choose among brands, stores, and styles for YOUR needs,

not theirs. Clothes shopping online can also be a savings as long as the return options are reasonable.
- Personal Environment Control – We all want to be cool in the summertime, and warm in the winter. Unfortunately, many people tend to set meat-locker temperatures in the summer and toaster oven conditions in the winter. Studies show this is not healthy - plus it can cost you dearly in utility expenses. To understand why, the heating and cooling systems we use are not linear from the standpoint of the thermostat setting. For instance, with central air, to maintain cooling at 77 degrees may take X amount of energy. Lowering it one degree will take X amount plus an additional Y. Lowering it another degree will require an additional Y plus Z, and so on. This why using a higher thermostat setting for the power-hungry central A/C and using ceiling fans and other area fans to move air is more cost-effective. The same physics also applies to winter heating.
- Transportation – The cost is not only the price of the vehicle. Add to that the financing cost, maintenance, insurance, title and tag costs, and fuel, and it climbs quickly. An enhanced vehicle is one that has more features and comforts than what is required for its purpose. Many times, these enhancements are no more than your succumbing to the intense marketing pressures aimed at you to 'upgrade' or 'enhance your lifestyle'. Also, generally speaking, the more expensive the base vehicle costs, the more expensive the 'support' costs will be.
- Communication – One of the confusions today is that a 'smartphone' is a communication device. This is not true! A smartphone is a portable data storage, communication, and computing system – it goes far beyond just 'communicating'. So, the question is, do you need to carry around this powerful data center with you just to talk to someone? The answer is no! While the practicality of a portable phone cannot be denied, a simple, reliable, and inexpensive 'feature' or flip phone will serve this purpose

well. The 'smartphone' generation has taken on the persona of a cult – you don't *need* this enhancement!
- Recreation – The modernist and commercial world want you to be involved in recreation and entertainment as it takes your mind off of the other miserable aspects of modernist life. No one claims that recreation or entertainment is a bad thing. The problem is that some recreation can become complex and expensive and have a net result of increasing stress, not reducing it. Use some critical thinking when it comes to these categories; does the NET result of recreation result in an increase in your stress and life complexity, or a desired reduction?

Now, let's look at some new categories that definitely fall into the *wants* area:

- Vacations – If you browse travel magazines, watch travel shows, and fix on the travel aspects of all news, you will want to become a 'traveler'. Some people make this a major part of their lives, with stickpins on a world map. No doubt, it is enjoyable seeing famous places, meeting other nationalities and enjoying beautiful surroundings, but exotic vacations can be expensive and stressful in the planning and implementation. A yearly vacation of reasonable length, to places that are single non-stop trips and little language barrier, may be a more balanced goal. A vacation trip should be a special event, not a contest with your peers and family. See vacation substitutes under the 'Luddite Nuggets' chapter.
- Spa trips – Spa visits definitely do not come under the 'needs' category. Going to a Spa can be enjoyable, and in many cases, beneficial. However, living at a Spa can become a status symbol for some. This can be an expensive *want*.
- Shopping Mall Cruising – Mall visits for recreational purposes is akin to a mouse visiting a cat emporium. This is one of the most intense concentrations of modernist marketing influences. Do you think you can just 'look' and

- not wind up with more gadgets that you will have to make room for and eventually dispose of? Don't!
- Brand Name Clothing, Shoes, Jewelry – 'Brand Name' converts, in the minds of many, into 'quality'. In some cases this is true, but many times you have average to above-average quality and an 'image' promoted by powerful marketing forces using tools such as television, movies, print and online images, and celebrities (who are NOT Selective Luddites)!
- Expensive Restaurants – Expensive restaurants are the culinary equivalent of 'name brand' above. Regularly dining at such establishments can be costly, and it can subvert your appreciation of other meals - at home, at friends' homes, business meals, etc. Once you are used to 5-star presentations, unusual spices, and highly skilled chefs, it is harder to appreciate 'normal' fare. Save the expensive dining for special occasions.

Skewed Values –

Out of confusion of our needs and wants comes values that are skewed. This is inevitable because people develop such strong wants that the line between *needs* and *wants* becomes blurred. This not only adds unnecessary expenses to your family budget, but also more stress load.

How does this happen?

Younger family members (and some adult ones, to be honest) are easily influenced by their peers, mass media, and saturation marketing into purchasing 'things' that have a short life-span. This creates a desire to constantly keep up with the latest and greatest. Because it is a human tendency to not be wasteful, the oldest and *not* greatest become discarded and start taking up storage space and engendering confusion as to what the 'stuff' is for. Adopt an emigration plan to intelligently migrate the 'stuff' out of your life.

- Keep the replaced item for 30 days just for a backup in case the new item fails.

- If the old item has value worth retrieving, list it on Craigslist, eBay, or another outlet to sell (do NOT store it for a garage sale!).
- If the value is too low to be concerned with, then drop it off at Goodwill or a local charity outlet.
- If it is not suitable for Goodwill, then put it into the trash (the recycle bin).
- Use the '6-month rule'. If you haven't used an item, planned on using it, or thought about it in a six-month period, then start the above migration plan.

If you adopt this plan you can stop the accumulation of unneeded junk. It also gives you a 'green' peace of mind that the maximum utilization of manufactured items has been achieved, and a warm feeling that maybe someone less fortunate will have something they can use.

For younger members of the family it is helpful to provide education as to what goes into buying whims and impulse purchases, as well as 'testing' the item to determine if it really is a *need*. Here's a plan to control unholy desires for the 'latest' by family members.

- Bargaining works better than edicts and dictates. Have some bargaining chips – things kids want but don't yet have, activities that they are not allowed to do now but MAY be allowed to do in the future.
- Employ model jump. Instead of battling over the newest release of xyz, then agree to upgrade only every other release, or only model numbers that are odd or even, or the model numbers that can be evenly divided by 3, or – well you get the idea. This makes you onboard, and not a villain, and creates an anticipation in the child for 'their' upgrade release, etc. This simple plan can reduce your tech junk collection by at least half.

Keeping up with the Joneses.

This is one of the deadliest ways to becoming trapped like a fly in a spider web. The key to beating this is for all the family becoming educated so they don't *want* to keep up with the Joneses. This is difficult when friends and associates live in McMansions, drive 'brand' automobiles, wear designer clothing, belong to the country club, and have prestigious private schools for the kiddoes.

Of course, if you make the decision to down-size, you will most probably move OUT of the McMansion, and when you do, you will leave many of the other trappings of affluence that will act as a temptation. After this, it is just a matter of re-ordering your entire family's priorities. You have realized the inability of modernism to deliver happiness and recognize it as a life-style that is performing a slow *execution* on you and your family.

Speaking of family priorities, consider this: There is a single wage-earner that, because of unreasonable demands of family members to keep up with the Joneses, has to work long hours at the best paying job he can find (which will be a competitive environment contributing to stress), engages in long, stress-filled commutes, and then has to spend additional hours to maintain a respectably appearing residence. Because of the accumulated pressures to 'keep up with the Joneses', he one day prematurely checks out with a massive coronary. Is this a good trade-off for all the family members? Speaking of pressures…

High Stress –

The most insidious part of the modernist lifestyle is stress. While stress is a part of the human emotional makeup, it is there for short-term benefit. For example, if you are put in danger from animals, events, or other humans, the stress reflex kicks in the adrenalin and you are able to do things like scaling tall buildings and catching bullets in your palm.

The damage takes place when there is a prolonged low-grade stress. And, like the proverbial frog in boiling water, if we were dropped into the normal stress of modern life cold, we would react like a jumping frog. But, the stress has been building gradually over decades, to the point that we consider it normal and natural, not realizing the toll it is taking on our physical and emotional health.

So how can we handle stress? There are many self-help books on general stress management, and they can be helpful. Usually though, they do not fully address the causes of stress from a modernist environment, but use techniques to reduce your overall life stress while you *co-exist* with this environment. This is well and good, but let's look at the modernist lifestyle and the stress creators.

- Paperwork – Having many accounts that require paper based accounting and payments can be overwhelming because of the number of steps they require; receiving the paperwork, opening it, writing a paper check, mailing the paperwork and check back and hoping it doesn't get lost in the mail. Of course, many people today pay bills online. While this is certainly a time-saver, you just have to be sure that the payment portal is secure and you have a good audit record of your payment history. There a number of automated bill payment systems that can simplify this task even further. Bottom line though, is to do what you can to reduce the number of accounts you have to pay, either paper or online. What about multitudes of magazine and newspaper subscriptions? They all will pester you yearly for renewals. You don't need to keep up with all this – reduce your subscriptions to one or two most needed (if at all).
- Vehicle Maintenance – Numbers, numbers. You would think that the total maintenance items would be the items per vehicle times the number of vehicles – but it seems to be exponential for some reason. It is a fact that sometimes more than one vehicle per family is required, but examine a typical rolling stock inventory of many upwardly mobile modernists today:

    - Father's car
    - Mother's car
    - Teenage daughter's car
    - Teenage son's motorcycle
    - RV
    - Dual jet skis
    - Trailer for jet skis

- Bass boat
- Bass boat trailer

Keep in mind that almost every vehicle needs not only operational maintenance, but licenses, inspections, titles, tax assessments, storage, and insurance. Stress? Nah!

Solution? Obvious Man says to get rid of some of your rolling stock. However, many people consider it as recreational, and that's hard to surrender. The reason for having all of these obligations is due to being the *owner*. Ownership means the buck stops (and starts) with *you*. Alternatively, leasing and renting means other people take care of all of the headaches. Sure, you don't get to say you *own* an RV, but since an owned RV *sits* somewhere for the majority of the year, an RV rental makes a lot of sense. Many recreational toys can be leased or rented. Think outside the box!

- Work – Many employees, in the quest to obtain the best job and salary, do not examine the intangibles that go along with the position. Are the expectations of the employer that you are 100% dedicated to the company? Is 40hrs/week just the start – is future advancement dependent upon living at the office? Will you be working for supervisors that have no people management skills – will you be working with corporate psychopaths? Do you really not enjoy your position's responsibilities? These and other factors can raise the workplace stress to a high level. Solution? Soulful re-examination of how you want to make a living. Look at positions at smaller companies with lower pay but less hooks into your very being.
- Work commuting – Not only can you be stressed with the wrong job, if you live in the burbs you may have to make a long commute. This not only steals a few more hours of your life each day, but exposes you to accident possibilities, road rage, or vehicle breakdowns. All of these raise the stress you left work with by a few more degrees. The obvious solution is to downsize, require less salary, find a lower paying

position closer to you. If you want to be selective, however, some have elected to try to work four 10-hr days, or a variation, or to stay in apartments, motels, or other arrangements to reduce the number of commutes per week. You might find another workmate that wants to do the same that can share expenses and keep the costs low. This may or may not be a good solution depending upon your family makeup and obligations.

- Home maintenance – As if suffering through a stressful work environment and having a long and stressful commute home is not enough, you now have to contend with your home maintenance - like lawn mowing, flower beds, leaf raking, trash hauling, sidewalk and driveway cleaning, minor repairs, etc. Some of these can be contracted out but that expense means you must work more or longer to cover those expenses. If you look at yard care as an obligation and not a relaxation, then the best solution is being in a Condo or apartment.
- Technology overload – How many remote controllers do you have – can you adequately remember all of their features? How many smartphone and tablet accounts do you need to constantly pay for your entire family? How many electronic appliances and tools do you own that you would not be able to repair if needed? Would you be able to repair your car if you wanted to? Because of 'advanced technology', are you becoming increasingly in the dark with the common things you used to understand? Most can identify with these questions, and they show that the average person is becoming technologically overwhelmed. How do you counter this trend? By simplifying your 'things' and services that are technology based. Technology overload is a subtle condition and usually increases incrementally, each step hardly noticeable. It will take some discipline to roll back your stuff from wants to needs. A good example is an automatic washing machine. The earliest models had a motor, transmission, water pump, and a simple electro-mechanical timer to perform all of the steps. Today's latest offerings have more computer power than we used to have

on our desktops not too many years ago. They can do almost everything except cook your supper, and yet both models basically do one thing – wash your clothes. The difference is that the older models could actually be repaired by the owner, the newest models – good luck with that! The early model was a *need*, the latest model, because of the power of marketing, is a *want*.

- Unfulfilled Goals – Being in the modernist snare can modify many of your goals in life. The power of marketing can entice you to purchase and use more and newer things that can upset your financial goals. They can also suck up much of your excess time so that goals that need time to pursue are no longer viable. One of your goals may be to have a functional, loving family arrangement. That goal can be compromised when family members each go their own way into the modernist mold and become less functional, less loving, and lose the natural human interaction expected within a family unit. The loss of these and other goals creates stress in your life. The solution is to examine your goals, prioritize them, adopt the Selective Luddism techniques to help you reach them. Instead of stress, you can gain a measure of self-accomplishment and fulfillment!

The suggestions in this chapter cover the basic actions you can take to exit the 'progress' train. These actions can save you money, reduce your stress level, up the quality of your life, and buy you a lot of additional time. However, this would be of no benefit if your health was compromised, or you spent all of your money and time savings on medical issues. While you may not believe your personal health applies, many Luddite choices may require you to have a measure of good health. The following chapter provides more guidance on how to apply Selective Luddism on these important areas.

Chapter 8 Jumping Even Further

At the beginning of the previous chapter I asked a couple of questions that have not yet been addressed:

- What can I do to improve my diet, control my weight, and have more energy and better health?
- How can I avoid the medical treadmill?

Before we can be fully Selective Luddites and totally jump from the 'progress' train, we have to address these questions, as they are very much influenced by modernist practices. I detailed these issues in my previous book, 'Clueless 101, A Life Manual for Millennials', so am going to be using an abbreviated version of this information, but from a Selective Luddite viewpoint.

The areas that follow are:

- Fast food
- GMO
- Food labeling
- Contamination
- Factory foods
- Medical Care – Preventive
- Medical Care - Treatment

Fast Food

Fast food has been around for some time now. By definition, a fast food 'restaurant' is a place where you may purchase standardized food and be able to drive through and take delivery without leaving your vehicle. Most fast food establishments also have indoor seating. And, most fast food restaurants are part of a nationwide chain, either corporate owned, or franchised.

So why is fast food a concern? Let's examine some facts about the industry.

- Since the fast food chain presents a common menu at all stores in the chain, there have to be controls in place to accomplish this. They include:
    - Standardized serving sizes
    - Identical appearances
    - Inventories of all items on the menu
    - Warehousing capabilities
    - Mass shipping capabilities
    - Optimized ingredient life

    One can see that this degree of management takes a substantial corporate infrastructure – one that is reproducible throughout various areas of the country or world. In addition, the physical stores must have near identical equipment for preparing and serving the products, and identical training for store personnel. The food products that are processed and warehoused may have additives for the sole purpose of long shelf life and efficient distribution. With all of the required steps, the actual food becomes a secondary part of the process.
- Marketing – along with the distribution accomplishments, the marketing of the product is all-important. These businesses use massive advertising to convince potential customers to choose their product over the competition. This adds a premium to the product base price - so to be competitive, cost control and reduction is paramount. Much of this marketing is not addressing *needs* but focuses on *wants* – definitely a modernist practice!
- Appeal – Along with cost, competition requires that a fast food business has a great *tasting* product. So, if flavor enhancers can accomplish this, then great! If adding sugar or other sweeteners to the products enhances the taste, then add it! Within limited boundaries, it is almost carte blanche to do whatever can be done to 'food' to make the flavor be the one thing that lingers in a customer's memory. A lot of research at the fast food corporate laboratories is done for just this purpose.

- The nature of 'fast' food eating is fast and on-the-run. This is not the best condition for maintaining your health or keeping your weight in check.

If you want to help your health, do NOT make fast food establishments your constant source of nourishment. Learn to cook certain easy meals, even ones you can take with you to work. Use fast food for real emergencies or consider it a 'treat' experience. However, just remember, the fast food industry is doing everything it can to make you addicted to their products – including clever advertising, enhancing flavors, creating peer pressure, and promoting 'convenience'.

GMO

One of the most controversial developments today is 'genetically modified organisms', or GMOs. Why do we need GMOs and who is behind it? As usual, in areas like this, you have to follow the money. Where does the money come in? From big agriculture and the companies that supply them. It is caused by the idea that enough food to feed the world can no longer be provided by family run farms, and is a mainstay of zealous modernist thought. Whether that is true or not, the resulting solution is large farming efforts with high mechanization and replicable processes. The major components of this model are petroleum-based fertilizers, and a lot of pesticides and herbicides to control pests and weeds. In this process, you plant seeds, add ammonia fertilizers, irrigate when necessary, regularly spray with herbicides and pesticides, and then harvest with large scale harvesters. The only weak link is the crops themselves. They could not be guaranteed to survive heavy applications of poisons. What to do? Change the plants! So, seed company scientists developed seeds that produced plants crafted to be 'better' in that they could resist weed killers without themselves being killed. In a real creative victory, scientists developed corn that produced its own pesticide.

But, that is not the extent of GMO development. Many other seeds have been modified for better life-span, storage capability, and crop harvest. Agricultural lobbyists are working diligently to hide GMO labeling on food products-as currently it is required. So, if you choose to eliminate GMO based foods from your diet, you will have to research thoroughly. But what about fast food and other restaurant establishments-do you think they will be as diligent as you with their ingredient selections?

Food Labeling

Want to have an amusing pastime? Then play the 'guess what's in your groceries' game. In the past this game hardly existed. After all, you would go out to the garden, pick a tomato or dig up a potato and what you had was...a tomato and a potato! Unfortunately, because of modernist progress, we have 'advanced' since those days and we seldom get those *single name* foodstuffs. Foods you may find in your local supermarket have been prepackaged and will have a few, to many, many ingredients added to enhance the flavor, preserve it, color it, and add missing 'nutrients' that in many cases got removed in the initial processing. You can see what has been added to your food by reading the package under 'Ingredients'. The order is supposed to represent the quantity from the first listed ingredient (the most) to the last. Why should you be interested in doing this? After all, the product tastes good and it fills you up, right? The reason is that some of these added ingredients have now been found to be *unhealthy*, and it would be really nice for YOU, the consumer, to know and understand which ones are included.

The companies know this, and they do all that they legally can to hide or obfuscate their ingredient list so that it doesn't impact sales. You're probably wondering why a food packager would do this??? The answer may shock you – they are large corporations with stockholders looking for a return on their investments, run by highly paid CEOs that gain huge bonuses by making their company profitable, and that employ worker bees just doing their jobs – jobs that include creating foodstuffs that can capture market share by using all of the food science tricks at their disposal. Even though at times you must use their products, you can be smart and selective. YOU are the one that has to keep them honest by deciphering the ingredients list. Don't depend upon the government to protect you as there is a steady *shuttling* from food company to government oversight departments, and back to food companies. Additionally, there are constantly new steps being taken to hide even further the makeup of your food. Be diligent on this!

Contamination

Not to be overshadowed by the inclusion of unwanted ingredients, we have another source of contamination. However, instead of the packaged foods, it is in the fresh produce and meat and dairy products. Don't feel like you are in a shooting gallery, but here are the issues in this category:

- Truck farm produce – Fresh produce from 'truck farms' has been found to contain bacteria, viruses, and parasites on multiple occasions. This contamination can come from unsanitary conditions in the harvesting or handling by workers. This can be anywhere from the field to the grocery store employees. To decontaminate produce at home, fill a large bowl with water and add a few tablespoons of food grade hydrogen peroxide. After soaking for 15-20 minutes, rinse it with water.
- Chicken – Factory produced chicken can be from chickens that are fed mass-produced food, kept in crowded conditions where fecal droppings collect, and consequently, because of the unsanitary conditions, require antibiotics to be added to their food or water. This means much of the chicken offered in the supermarket will have or have had antibiotics unless the packaging says there have been none added (but how can we ever know?). The contamination that the antibiotics are supposed to address can creep into the actual processing of the chickens themselves. Here are the precautions to observe with chicken meat:
    - Always wash the raw chicken before preparation.
    - Do not re-use knives, plates, or cutting boards after using them on chicken.
    - Always make sure the chicken is fully cooked.
    - Look for range-raised, no antibiotics used, and no growth hormones.
- Eggs – Some of the precautions pertaining to handling of chicken also applies to eggs. Wash the eggs before using as poor packaging may leave pathogens on the egg shell. Look

- for eggs from chickens that are free-range and no antibiotics, etc. added.
- Beef – The main concern with beef products are growth hormones and antibiotics. Also, there can be contamination introduced in the processing plant or butcher shop while preparing the cuts.
- Pork – The same concerns for beef and chicken also apply to pork. Additionally, you must thoroughly cook pork so as to kill any Trichinella cysts or larvae that could be present.[9]
- Fish – The types and amounts of contamination vary depending on the type fish and how it is harvested. Ocean harvested fish have been found with concentrations of lead, mercury, PCBs, and other contaminants. The higher on the food chain, the greater the risk of contamination, as it accumulates in the flesh before being eaten by a larger predator. Consequently, a concern would be large fish like shark, swordfish, and tuna. It can be Ok to eat these periodically, just don't make them a staple. It would seem that farm-raised fish would be a safer bet since there is a more controlled environment. A problem that has been found, however, is that runoff from agricultural fields with pesticides and fertilizers, and lead and PCBs from industrial processing, can collect in the fish ponds and contaminate the fish.

Some seafood products imported from third-world countries may not have adequate safeguards against pollution. This is especially true in places where there are unregulated and unpoliced industrial processes among fish and shrimp farms. Just look closely and research the origin of these types of products.

Factory Foods

One of the worst modernist 'advances' in food marketing is what I term 'factory foods'. I know most processed and packaged foods are produced in factories – and some of these are beneficial. What I am referring to are products that have been designed by food scientists, created using a few base foods (mainly flours and legumes), and then enhancing these cheaper bulk ingredients by including a host of additives to achieve desired results. Consideration is given to consistency, color, flavor, aroma, the ability to be easily manufactured, and a long shelf life. The vast majority of 'snack foods' are factory foods. Those aromatic goodies at service stations and many fast food establishments are factory foods. If you want to find out more, research food science, the food additives trade shows, and the profession of a food scientist. If you are trying to become healthier, eliminate factory foods from your diet. If you are trying to control your weight, eliminate factory foods from your diet.

Quick Checklist

Not all bad foods are foods. Some of them are items that by themselves will not sustain life. And ingesting many of them can make you quite ill. Some of these will be in the following list, along with 'food' items that you should avoid.

- What do you drink all day long? If you are slugging down sodas, then STOP! Find an alternate like sparkling waters if you crave fizzes, otherwise herbal teas, certain fruit drinks and just plain water to quench thirst.
- Do NOT drink diet drinks with Aspartame, Sucralose, Acesulfame or Saccharin. Xylitol from Birch trees, and Stevia are preferred sweeteners.
- Look at buying natural flavor concentrates at a health food store and use with good quality sparkling waters to substitute for soft drinks. Eliminate the sodas in your diet!
- Avoid any foods or drinks that have corn syrup, high fructose corn syrup, fructose, dextrose, white or brown sugar. If you must use sugar in moderation, choose raw cane sugar rather than sugar-beet processed sugar. Better yet, use honey, pure maple syrup (not artificial), and organic Agave for sweeteners.
- MSG is a flavor enhancer that is added to foods to enhance the flavor by tricking your taste buds. It has been found to cause a number of health issues. Because food producers know this, it is sometimes disguised as *Natural Meat Tenderizer, Natural Flavors, or Monosodium Glutamate,*

to name a few (see a full list at http://lifespa.com/sneaky-names-for-msg-check-your-labels/).
- Don't use lard or other hydrogenated fats for cooking. Instead, try hazelnut, olive, flaxseed, coconut, or sunflower. Do your research to find the pros and cons for each choice.
- While olive oil is one of the best all-around oils, many olive oil blends are adulterated with other oils. Research a good source of certified olive oil.
- Do not consume any food containing Trans Fats, artificial food dyes, or other chemicals.
- Avoid meats with sodium nitrate and nitrite, potassium bromate, sulfur dioxide, sodium sulfite and BHA and BHT.
- Avoid plastic containers made of BPA. For many years, cans have had a BPA-based lining. Avoid canned foods unless you can ascertain that they do not have BPA linings.
- Instead of buying 'drinking' water in plastic bottles, consider a glass or stainless container you can carry water in. Obtain a good quality water filter to use to fill your container.

Here are the most important points about food and your diet: Life-giving food is not food just because it *tastes* good. It has been *designed* to taste good by the food scientists working at the corporate food factories! Life-giving food is not food just because it fills you up! The food industry, through clever marketing, will do all they can to make you feel *full*. You can eat tasty 'food' that fills you up and results in a disease-plagued life - one propped up by an eager medical industry and opportunistic drug producers - until you prematurely die. Not surprisingly, this type of 'progress' can be laid at the feet of food modernists.

Medical Care – Prevention

No one can deny that being healthy is in one's best interest. However, there's a lot of disagreement on what health really is and how to achieve it. Until we all reach the Singularity, it is still an accepted part of life that we will eventually break down and cease functioning. However, we don't have to speed that rendezvous along by a lack of preventative health habits.

When you were born, unless you had a genetic problem or your mother had a health issue, you were the healthiest of your life. All your parts worked properly and until outside influences came into play, you were in (relatively) perfect health. Unfortunately, in these early years your health was not in your hands (or maybe fortunately) - your parents or caretakers controlled your health environment. The factors that contributed to your health were your genetics, your environment, your immune system, and your diet. Although you have no control over your genetics, the other factors, your environment, immune system and diet can be controlled. So, if you are currently living in an acceptable environment, you are left with two important factors that affect your health; your *immune system*, and your *diet*. YOU can affect these. This explains why the general health level in the so-called civilized world is deteriorating, with young people becoming obese and contracting 'diseases' that just decades ago were almost unheard of, or were not even considered diseases – people are NOT managing these two factors.

Since we have already covered food, the following are other areas you need to be concerned with:

- If you are trying to control your weight, diets and dieting can be only temporarily effective – you will need to modify your behavior. This modification includes learning about your body and how it works. It will also require that you learn some basics about food and nutrition.
- Start with a simple truth that few food manufacturers, processors, or vendors have your health in mind. The first concern is profits – your health is a bonus if it fits into the marketing of products.
- Add to this the fact that many of the watchdog organizations, whether industries, medical, or governmental, are not overseeing your health. Many of these are obscene entanglements of drug companies, medical associations, medical schools, doctors' associations and governmental agencies that are supposed to watch over

- your health. Do NOT trust them – YOU must watch over your health!
- Do NOT use fast food restaurants as your main food source – only in emergencies!
- Try to refrain from living on foods that are produced in factories.
- Disease prevention is the combination of the proper nutrients that you take in, and maintaining a strong immune system. Study the immune system chemistry and what you can do to strengthen it.
- You should have at least a reasonable amount of exercise to keep your body functioning.
- Health supplements are a good practice as so much of our food is nutrient poor. While the basic vitamin supplements are OK, you might look at mineral supplements and phytonutrients. These used to come from healthy soils, but since much of the farmland today is deficient because of factory farming (a modernist development), it is beneficial to supplement.
- There is some serious human longevity improvement development in progress. The emphasis is on human 'health-span' not just 'life-span'. This means doing the things to enable you to have a healthy body for the longest time. This not necessarily modernist thinking, just some common-sense practices that don't take hi-tech machinery.

Immune system

A critical player in your preventative health is your immune system. While your immune system is operating optimally when you are an infant, the things you do, such as lifestyle and diet start a slow deterioration. The good news is that many older people have robust immune systems because they recognize how important it is and take steps to strengthen it.

What does your immune system do for your health? Through various systems and processes, your immune system attacks pathogens that invade your body through various pathways. This process can be your best prevention ally, and will be active during sickness in a curative phase. Strong immune systems can keep you from succumbing to the normal maladies that many suffer from and help you conquer them quickly. There are many activities that can compromise your immune system and many others that can strengthen it, including certain foods, herbs, and other nutrients. If there is anything worth intensive study to help your health, the immune system is it.

Medical Care - Treatment

Everyone should do everything they realistically can to *prevent* sickness - as the alternative is not a good trip. Once you have a broken-down body, you will be forced to hand it over to an almost dysfunctional healthcare system. Why is it dysfunctional? Let's analyze briefly how this huge industry that encompasses over 17% of the US GDP functions. Here are the players:

- Doctors, nurses and medical specialists
- Hospitals
- Medical schools
- Medical Boards and associations
- Medical insurance companies
- Government

What are the roles of each of these participants?

Doctors, nurses, medical specialists

Doctors, nurses and other medical specialists are the ones that provide medical care and services to you, the patient. Doctors in past years used to go to medical school, get their degree, be certified, hang up their shingle and take patients. They were able to set their own charges, dispense advice and medicines that they thought were best. Their charges were reasonable and their overhead was low. What is the scene today? Doctors still go to school, but schools have changed (see reason below). They still graduate and are still are able to open an office (if they have deep pockets). However, setting their own rates is not as easy as it once was (for reason see insurance following). They also are more limited in what they can prescribe and the advice they can give (explanation following). This means that what should be a simple patient-doctor relationship has now become a complex interplay of multiple players with their own vested interests and agendas. If you haven't experienced this yet – you will! Do EVERYTHING to stay out of this web by exercising *good preventative care.*

Hospitals

Hospitals can be publicly or privately owned. The private ownership is usually a corporation formed with a number of doctors, business administrators and other specialists. All hospitals are highly regulated and must conform to sets of standards set by local, state, and federal agencies. No general hospital will stray outside of this highly complex box for fear of regulatory punishment and legal action.

Medical schools

Medical schools are specialized institutions for training doctors and supporting medical specialists. Most are four to six year curriculums with residency requirements. Once a medical student finishes all of the required courses with passing grades, they graduate and can be certified for practice. There is a huge influence that pharmaceutical companies have over not only the doctors and hospitals, but with the medical schools and the many teaching doctors. This influence naturally colors the curriculum and course material; e.g. medical diseases are best treated with drugs or surgery.

Medical Boards and Associations

Medical boards and associations certify medical graduates for the practice of medicine. If a doctor does not comply with legal and medical regulations, the associations have the power to sanction him or even remove his certification. If a doctor still practices medicine they will take the lead in prosecuting him. This is a good procedure if a doctor practices unsound and harmful medical procedures. The problem is, who decides what is unsound and harmful? Since the associations have close relations with government and medical supply companies (like drug companies), then one can see there can be possibilities for mischief.

Medical insurance companies

This category is one of the most unfathomable players of this unholy commune. One would think if there were to be 'gatekeepers' or throttles on rising medical expenses driven by greed and corruption, the insurance companies would be the ones, right? After all, they are paying the majority of the expenses in claims submitted by any of the medical providers.

You would think this until you analyze their business model. Medical insurance companies are regulated by insurance boards in the separate states. These boards, in addition to other regulations, approve the rate structures for their various insurance plans. If an insurance company is not making enough revenue to cover their cost of doing business, then they simply petition the boards for a rate increase. The boards examine audited financials of the company and if they agree (which they mostly do), allow the rates to be increased. In business, there is the term ROI, which means 'return on investment', or similarly 'return on expenses'. The model is that a company is guaranteed a return on their cost of doing business. If the cost goes up, the return goes up. As an example, if a company was permitted a 10% return on their costs, and their costs were $100, they would receive $10. If the costs doubled to $200 their return would be $20. This is a simplification, but the principle is true – and you can see why they are NOT the controllers of medical costs!

Government

So, if the doctors, hospitals, drug companies, and insurance companies are not the ones to bring fiscal sanity to runaway medical costs, then the answer has to be - *the government!* Sadly, if you have that conclusion, you are again wrong. While there have been sporadic attempts by government to control medical costs, most of these attempts result in laws creating more control, accountability, and penalties for what bureaucrats have spawned. As with any government endeavor to modify human behavior and large industries, the main result is increased costs and the inherent corruption that accompanies complex regulations and big money. That increased cost doesn't just evaporate; it gets passed down to whom? The patient (consumer) and taxpayer.

The more you examine the interrelationship between these groups, the more you find a massive resistant-to-improvement industry. It is using YOU for test subjects, YOU as funding for their huge economic activity, paying governmental 'watchdogs' for approval, and doing their best to pull the wool over YOUR eyes to keep you from discovering what they are up to.

Some think the solution is to eliminate private entities and have the government do it all (the so-called 'single-payer' solution). But, do you really think that millions of bureaucrats, thousands of lobbyists and corrupt governmental appointees can create a smoothly operating, effective and fair medical care system? Sure!

A better solution – for you!

There is a better solution for you personally. First, as mentioned earlier, do EVERYTHING to eliminate the possibility of being a permanent resident of the medical monster. If you have an accident, or are shot in a home invasion, then by all means hurry to the quickest hospital and doctor for treatment. This is a great reason to use the great medical resources we have available. However, with organic diseases and common deteriorating health issues, you have alternative solutions available, which many Selective Luddites feel are superior. Here is just a sampling:

- Co-op medical plans and care
- Faith-based medical plans
- Naturopathy, acupuncture
- Massage and total body manipulation
- Subscription medical care (contract with a doctor for a fixed fee)
- Buffet type medical practices (new)

The interesting thing about the above partial list is that overall, healthcare may be cheaper, but it will usually NOT be covered by your 'super' insurance plan. The 'standard' medical care insurance has substantial costs added to it because of the insurance and governmental reporting requirements, plus no incentive for cost reduction.

This book is not intended to make specific recommendations for you personally, but to educate you on how things really are, get you thinking out of the box, and motivate you to become educated so you can make the best decisions for yourself and your family and friends. This is what being a Selective Luddite is all about.

Here's something to think about. There are a half dozen spots around the world where people live unusually long and healthy lives. In contrast, the citizens in some of the most advanced countries in history suffer from some of the worst health conditions (and shortened lives) ever recorded. Why is this? It's not because of some pandemic caused by a mosquito or Ebola-like virus. No, there are differences, but you have to examine the environment, living conditions and diet of the people in these areas.

Don't be confused what healthcare is. It is NOT superior health insurance plans. These are just a means to compensate all of the medical industry players, and insurance 'health care' discussions have been a subterfuge to hide the real truth. Health care is the totality of the decisions you make about diet, lifestyle, exercise, supplements, and preventative health actions. It also includes the treatment decisions *you* choose in case of serious disease or injury. Remember, a great insurance policy will NOT make you healthy!

Conclusion

Exiting a speeding train can be done several ways: waiting until the next stop, making a dive and a graceful roll, or hopping onto the back of a horse a friend is riding alongside the train. Any which way, the goal of getting off the train is accomplished. It may not be an easy or elegant exit, but Selective Luddites feel strongly about where the train is heading and fervently believe they don't want to continue *that* trip.

Chapter 9 Mapping Out a New Path

From the preceding chapter, we can create a 'punch-list' of things to do and to avoid on our quest to become a Selective Luddite.

Do's:

- Honestly examine your current lifestyle – identify the areas that make you unhappy, stressed, or broke.
- If Selective Luddism seems like the answer, identify the modernist areas that you can target to benefit you and your family. Attempt to eliminate the rest.
- Have an intelligent family discussion of the areas that can be addressed.
- Think outside the box – instead of just some incremental tweaks in your current lifestyle, broaden your view. It may be time to make some major decisions that could result in a sweeping elimination of many modernist ills.

Don'ts:

- Don't immediately go full-bore Selective Luddism – make gradual changes with evaluations of the change for effectiveness.
- Don't force Luddite changes on the family – for Selective Luddism to work, each family member must be onboard, realizing the good to be gained.
- Don't go 'primitive' just because it may seem romantic or exotic.
- Don't throw out good technology just because it's tech – it might be a life simplification over some other solution.
- Don't brainwash yourself on what are really *needs* and *wants* just because of that *special* 'want'.

With all of the information that's been presented, you can make a couple of choices.

Embrace the modern world, flow with the other flotsam and jetsam down the 'progress' river, and have faith that the powers that are in charge have everything in hand (do you REALLY think this?).

But if this is your choice, be aware that your life will be more complex and busier than it need be, you could wind up living payday-to-payday, a major portion of your waking moments will be nothing but career, your family could become fragmented and dysfunctional, stress will be your constant companion, and you have a good possibility that you will die sooner than your Selective Luddite neighbors.

Or, you can become a Selective Luddite. There is nothing to sign, no physical exam is needed, and there are absolutely *no membership fees!*

With your Selective Luddite membership, you have full rights of decision-making as it pertains to the quality of *your* life. Being a 'Selective' member means that you may pick and choose only those 'features' of modernist living that make sense, improve the quality of your life, save you money, and reduce your overall stress and mental load. The rest can be thrown into the Selective Luddite trashcan.

The 'Selective' in Selective Luddism means that you can make your own decisions about the level of modernist practices in your life.

You may make a large Selective Luddite change, or you may elect to make a few 'tweaks' to incrementally improve your life. Be aware that in all probability, this decision will not noticeably change the timeframe of *when* the exponential endpoint of 'progress' will happen, *what* it will be, or whether your neighbors convert into singularity beings. However, the main thing to keep in mind is that you can step aside from the train *and* track to the extent you wish.

Chapter 10 Important Addendum

When I started this book, I was pretty neutral in my beliefs about how modernism is affecting the younger generations (millennials and their progeny). However, during my research into other modernist areas, I kept discovering sobering reports of the results of the marriage of technology and the current crop of young people. You might say I originally took the view that the jury was still out on this issue. I no longer think this – I now feel the jury has returned to the courtroom and the verdict is *not good*. To explain my concerns, let's examine a number of different areas that are pertinent.

Addiction

People become addicted to any number of things: drugs, alcohol, food, gambling, and pornography, to name a few. The degree of addiction can be measured by the effects that a withdrawal from the addicted item can have on the individual. By this measure, there is little doubt that addiction to technology is strongly present among young people. See these links:

http://www.telegraph.co.uk/technology/news/8436831/Student-addiction-to-technology-similar-to-drug-cravings-study-finds.html
https://www.addiction.com/addiction-a-to-z/technology-addiction/
http://virtual-addiction.com/technology-addiction/
http://www.healthline.com/health/addiction/gaming-and-technology#Overview1
http://www.dailymail.co.uk/news/article-3785511/Chinese-man-threatens-jump-25th-floor-balcony-lost-iPhone-6.html

Physical Harm – Posture

Recent reports by medical specialists have shown that prolonged use of a smartphone or tablet held at a stomach to chest level can cause structural deterioration of the upper spine and neck. Obviously, with random intermittent use, there would be little problem. Young people's use of these devices for hours on end, however, can result in possible damage. In addition to the neck and spine, it has also been reported that great amounts of texting can cause problems with the thumbs and fingers.

http://www.cbsnews.com/news/omg-youre-texting-your-way-to-back-pain/
http://www.goodhousekeeping.com/health/wellness/a24269/smartphone-syndromes/
https://www.sciencedaily.com/releases/2013/09/130905160452.htm

Physical Harm – Eyesight

Eye deterioration can result from prolonged fixed and constant focus. It does not allow your eyes to exercise the muscles used for focusing. Focusing on small smartphone screens at a fixed distance for hours and hours is eventually going to become problematic.

http://www.bbc.co.uk/newsbeat/article/26780069/smartphone-overuse-may-damage-eyes-say-opticians
http://www.livescience.com/15009-smartphone-affects-vision.html
http://www.digitaltrends.com/mobile/does-your-phone-damage-your-eyes-an-experts-advice/

Physical Harm – Muscle Tone and Weight Gain

The older concerns about muscle health and weight control were focused more on sedentary behaviors using a computer at a desk. Yep, still have that, but now we can add other concerns. See here:

http://www.livestrong.com/article/46320-obesity-children-technology/
https://consumer.healthday.com/mental-health-information-25/behavior-health-news-56/your-smartphone-may-be-making-you-fat-678341.html

Deterioration of Communication Abilities

There are many different factors that make up communication. Meaningful vocabulary is important, but equally important are eye contact and body language. Research indicates that these two things make up around 93% of total communication. The danger for young people is that, because they are adopting electronic communication at an early age, they will not be learning how to fully integrate all these factors to communicate adequately.

http://www.nydailynews.com/life-style/texting-ruining-art-conversation-fear-losing-ability-traditional-face-to-face-conversations-article-1.1089679
http://www.npr.org/templates/story/story.php?storyId=126117811
http://www.prdaily.com/Main/Articles/4_ways_texting_is_killing_our_communication_skills_13330.aspx

Harm to Interpersonal Relationships

This is a sad category to even highlight. Young people at impressionable ages are adopting 'smart' technology instead of socialization skills. While strong parenting may offset some of this, many parents today don't have the knowledge or incentive to work this hard. It is a sobering thought to see what society reaps when these young people become older and are forced to interact with humans.

http://www.scientificamerican.com/article/how-your-cell-phone-hurts-your-relationships/
http://www.cnn.com/2013/01/10/health/kerner-social-relationship/index.html
http://theweek.com/articles/472326/how-cell-phone-wrecks-relationships--even-when-youre-not-using

Sleep Disorders

There are many factors that contribute to sleep disorders. However, along with all of the traditional causes, we joyfully add some new ones - the wonderful modernist gadgets that interfere with our physical and mental functions. Here are just a few of many references:

http://psychcentral.com/news/2015/02/03/smartphones-tied-to-poor-sleep-in-teens/80697.html
https://www.sciencedaily.com/releases/2013/06/130603163610.htm
http://sleepdisorders.dolyan.com/cell-phones-and-sleep-disorders/

Immune and Other Health Problems

Think that technology cannot negatively impact our health? Young people are especially susceptible:

http://www.telegraph.co.uk/science/2016/09/03/modern-life-is-killing-our-children-cancer-rate-in-young-people/
http://www.medicaldaily.com/5-reasons-why-cellphones-are-bad-your-health-247624

Distraction While 'Computing'

Do you think this means just texting and driving? Ha! There's more!

http://www.distraction.gov/stats-research-laws/facts-and-statistics.html
http://www.nsc.org/learn/NSC-Initiatives/Pages/distracted-driving-research-studies.aspx
http://www.cdc.gov/Motorvehiclesafety/Distracted_Driving/index.html
http://researchnews.osu.edu/archive/distractwalk.htm

It becomes apparent that any one of these practices is undesirable. However, a combination of many of them means young people may experience some serious problems that will have to be addressed at some future time. Some of them will be hard to reverse. What is a Selective Luddite to do?

- If you are a young person immersed in modernist technology, then research on your own what I have presented so that you convince yourself of the dangers. If you can't go cold-turkey elimination, then make a schedule, break up your use, deep-six the silly time-wasting games and social media life, take fewer 'selfies' and uploads of

trivia such as pictures of what you had for dinner, etc. Create a goal for withdrawal so you can make measurable gains. Don't let modernist values and rampant technology ruin your life!
- If you are a parent or parents of young children, then your task becomes more difficult as you become party to an 'us' vs 'them' struggle. The 'them' is your children's peers, school, recreation, and immersive marketing targeted to their culture. This is a formidable array of powerful forces to contend with. The solution is education and role modeling, showing and voicing the benefits you are enjoying. Sell, sell, sell Selective Luddism!

I have added this addendum because if there is a single reason to adopt Selective Luddism and you are a parent, then saving your children is it! Remember, your children are in your charge. Even though it may not seem like it at times, you also have authority over not just their physical health, but their mental. You will be resisted, but if you prevail, someday your children will stand out, and be head and shoulders above their peers.

Chapter 11 Luddism Nuggets

The following are Luddisms that haven't been covered in the previous chapters. These can be helpful no matter what level of Selective Luddism you choose to exercise.

Cost Savings

Smart devices – One of your on-going modernist costs is your smartphone, tablet, or other devices attached to the cellular network. The reason they are 'smart' is because they are connected wirelessly to the internet – the cost of which the cell companies pass on to you. How can you reduce the data charges? There are several ways:

- Just need to talk and maybe text? Dump the smartphone and get an inexpensive feature phone. You can save $20-50 per month.
- Cancel the data function on your plan (if possible and the phone is not on contract).[10] This allows you to use your paid off smartphone as a telephone, and if you have access to wi-fi, use the 'smart' functions over the wi-fi connection.
- Leverage other devices. Example: you have two smartphones and a tablet on a data plan. Keep the primary phone on data, remove it from the other devices. Then turn on the 'hotspot' or 'internet sharing' on your phone whenever you want internet access. Your other devices can connect to the phone via a local wi-fi connection. Be aware all three devices share your data plan, so don't go hog wild.

Utilities – Any energy saving systems or products, to be Selective Luddite qualified, should be simple, reliable, and cost-effective. This may rule out some 'sexy' solutions that may only be cost-saving after 10 or 20 years.

- Do you have natural gas to your home? You should be using a gas water heater, kitchen stove, clothes dryer, and

central heat. If you have a central unit that is a heat pump, use area gas heaters for your main heating and the heat-pump as a supplemental heat source.
- If your central air conditioning is an older unit with a SEER rating of 13 or less, consider an upgrade to a newer unit with SEER ratings of 22-28. These units can pay for themselves in 1-2 years. This suggestion is obviously for a home you own.
- Replace all of your lighting with LED bulbs – they are less expensive to operate and have longer lives.
- Look at installing radiant barriers, either film or paint, in your attic to cut down on radiant heating.
- If your attic insulation is minimum thickness or older technology, blow in some of the newer insulation so as to increase your R-factor. This will not only give you a more comfortable home in both summer and winter, but will greatly reduce your utility costs.

Home mortgages – If you own your home, are paying too much on your mortgage, and you have no place to down-size to, there may still be several things you can do:

- What is the interest rate on your current mortgage? If it is over the current offered rate plus approximately 2%, then you may be a candidate for a mortgage refinance. If so, make sure to have pre-payment clauses, so you can pay at your option on the principal, for a faster pay-down. While a 15yr term is enticing for the money savings and debt length, having a 30yr term with principal payment option allows you more freedom if your financial status changes (you could still pay it off in 15yrs if you chose to, with the same savings).
- Have you checked with your tax offices that you have all the exemptions you are entitled to? These are homestead, senior, veterans, disabilities, agricultural, and school tax relief. Any can make an impact on your monthly payment.
- Comparative shop your property insurance. It can vary from company to company. Also, look at bundling a home policy with your auto insurance for possible savings.

Transportation – Transportation costs are usually the second highest monthly obligation you will have, following your mortgage. So, savings here can impact your monthly financial expenses. Here are some options to look at:

- If you are a full-time urban dweller, you may choose to not have an automobile, depending instead on buses, subways, cabs, and Uber. While living in a straight urban setting may not be the best housing choice for a Selective Luddite lifestyle, if this is your choice and you selectively apply other features to reduce your modernist environment, then these will be your better choices. If the climate and city infrastructure supports it, bicycling can also be added.
- If you are a suburban dweller and you cannot currently make the changes to eliminate the commuting insanity, then examine some changes to save you money and provide other benefits.
  - Carpooling – has been around for a long time. It can work if you keep the 'pool' to 2 or 3. This will also reduce the mileage on your family car so that you are not inclined to buy a second, cheaper car to wear out with commuting use (against all Selective Luddite principles).
  - Research if there is a public transportation service available for the final part of your commute. If so, you can drive or carpool to the terminal area, where you may park free or cheaply, ride into the urban terminus where you can have a short walk to the office. While this may not seem like a simplifying exercise, the big gain is the elimination of expensive urban parking and more intense traffic.

Clothing – Clothing is a great target to address to reduce your living expenses, if you can be flexible in your viewpoints. First order of business, examine the minimalist practices on clothing. Also, flee from high-end clothing shops that deal in 'designer' brands. If you really want to get aggressive, start shopping at resale shops. There you will find quality clothing that, even though pre-owned, is in excellent shape and offers great savings.

Stress management

Modernists take vacations for 'relaxation' and 'stress relief'. However, even though certain vacations may qualify, most involve planning, financing, scheduling, the occasional missteps like missed flights, lost funds, becoming lost, etc, etc. On the stress ledger sheet, this may not be a good entry. Suggestions:

- If you own your home and you have already downsized, look at making a 'pocket garden' in your yard. This small garden can be lush, exotic, and have the accruements you might have in a vacation setting (tables, chairs, benches, bar, umbrellas, pond and stream, wind chimes, exotic signage, etc.). This can be your 'mini' vacation space – a place to easily go to relax and unwind. Keep external modernist influences out – this needs to be your island! The thought here is to have a 'vacation' at your home at any time you choose without having to go somewhere with the accompanying stresses.
- Scout out your local area for secluded, low-key places to stay for 3-day weekends. Perhaps a bed and breakfast with local gardens, lake, streams, etc. Look for something within a 1 to 1½hr drive.
- Research how the environment for your senses can affect your stress level. Certain aspects of Feng Shui can make for a relaxing environment. Many sounds have been recognized as stress relieving - water, distant storms, ocean waves, chimes, wind, even the ticking of a pendulum clock. Certain fragrances relieve stress – examine some aromatherapy products.
- Many people use meditation, yoga, and massage for stress relief. A weekly massage schedule may be a good investment.

Downsizing

'Downsizing' is a relative concept, not one size fits all. In the Selective Luddite universe, any downsizing is good, but if you are thinking downsizing is going from a 5-bedroom penthouse suite to a 4-bedroom penthouse suite, then you're not going to qualify for Selective Luddism membership. Downsizing is going through a transformation process in housing, as well as other lifestyle choices.

Some Selective Luddites stop at a minimalist level, whereas some shoot for a period environment, where they copy all of the trappings from say, the 1890's or the 1920's. Whatever your target may be, a small incremental downsize may not be worth the trouble. Check this topic further in the Luddite Examples chapter.

Young People

While most Selective Luddism candidates will be middle-aged or older (and NOT because they are not intelligent or 'cool'), there are a minority of the younger generations (gen Y and gen Z) that somehow have prematurely gained wisdom. These are seeing some cracks appearing in the modernist façade – especially the targeting of young people for the engine to fuel the 'progress' agenda.

If you are part of these younger generations, don't feel out of place. After all, Ned Ludd was a young man!

Being a potential Selective Luddite, your youth gives you an advantage – you have the energy and a longer lifespan to enjoy the benefits of applying the information in this book. So, kudos to you, and keep on learning and applying Selective Luddism principles!

Also....

To become an even wiser young person, and better equip yourself for a Selective Luddite life, please check out my previous book, 'Clueless 101, A Life Manual for Millennials'. You can find it on Amazon and other book dealers.

Chapter 12 Real Life Luddite Examples

What follows are actual Selective Luddism implementations. These may not showcase all of the various facets we have covered in this book, but are examples of some major areas.

Not everyone loves technology, even though they may be addicted to it.

Technology Addiction:
https://www.buzzfeed.com/markcmarino/why-iam-giving-up-technology-for-a-weekand-tw-12dly
https://www.wired.com/2010/09/should-you-give-up-gadgets-for-a-day/
http://www.businessinsider.com/i-failed-to-give-up-my-phone-for-a-week-2016-7/#day-2-monday-2

Some young people 'get it':
http://newyork.cbslocal.com/2016/08/22/stories-from-main-street-teenage-girl-ditches-smartphone-for-flip-phone-to-find-peace/

Downsizing can be just a simple move to a smaller, less expensive house. To *really* downsize, examine some of the newer trends in the following links. A major advantage to downsizing to a 'tiny home' is that it forces additional lifestyle changes that are beneficial Selective Luddite targets. You can't cheat when you want to keep a 500 sq. ft. walk-in closet (and all the clothes to fill it) and have a 400 sq. ft. tiny home!

Rural Towns - Finding New Life with Tiny Homes:
http://www.spurfreedom.org/

Directory of Tiny Home Communities:
http://tinyhousetalk.com/communities/

Retiree Choices:
http://www.aarp.org/livable-communities/housing/info-2015/tiny-houses-are-becoming-a-big-deal.html

On Land or Water:
http://tinyhousetalk.com/category/house-boats/
http://buildahouseboat.com/build-a-floating-house/

Off-Grid Living:
http://www.wikihow.com/Live-off-the-Grid
http://www.off-grid.net/
https://offgridworld.com/
http://www.countryfarm-lifestyles.com/off-grid.html#.V9Ie-q2lzkE
http://www.mnn.com/lifestyle/responsible-living/stories/going-off-the-grid-why-more-people-are-choosing-to-live-life-un
http://www.trueactivist.com/15-tips-for-going-off-grid-do-what-you-love-stop-being-a-debt-slave/

In an RV:
http://rvlife.com/
http://www.your-rv-lifestyle.com/RV-Life.html
http://www.heathpadgett.com/29-reasons-living-in-an-rv-is-better-than-living-in-a-house/
http://www.your-rv-lifestyle.com/

Sometimes, downsizing involves merely escaping suburbia or urban life. Moving to a smaller town has numerous advantages, from substantial cost savings to a sense of community and a more relaxing lifestyle. If you can find a small town within an hour's drive of a major urban center, this can still give you access to big city services you might desire. Try to stay in the 15,000 to 50,000 population size, although smaller communities can still work. This size can provide many of the services of the larger urban centers. Try for one that is not a massive visitor or traffic magnet. Also, be sure that city services and law enforcement are of high quality.

Quaint Small Towns:
http://www.countryliving.com/life/travel/g2294/must-visit-small-towns-across-america/
http://www.smithsonianmag.com/ist/?next=/travel/the-20-best-small-towns-in-america-of-2012-66120384/
http://www.foxnews.com/travel/2013/03/21/top-10-small-towns-in-america.html

Some of the home downsizing choices become more viable if you can work remotely. The following references provide information on remote employment. Remember, the better you have reduced your financial obligations by exercising Selective Luddism practices, the more remote positions qualify to support you.

Working Remotely:
https://www.fastcompany.com/3006402/7-great-reasons-encourage-working-remotely
http://www.techrepublic.com/blog/10-things/10-good-reasons-why-working-remotely-makes-sense/
http://www.howtoworkremotely.com/

I mentioned in an earlier chapter having a pocket garden can substitute for frequent vacation trips. There are, however, some recommendations if taking this route. Don't get over-ambitious – keep it small and manageable, design it so that it is not labor-intensive. Use borders, xeriscape plants, automatic drip watering, and choose vegetation that is for your planting zone. The goal is to make this a refuge for relaxation, not an obligation requiring excess work and creating stress.

Pocket Garden Designs:
http://www.houzz.com/pocket-garden
http://diyhomedesignideas.com/garden/small.php
https://www.yardapes.com/ornamental-gardens/
http://www.renegadegardener.com/index.htm?content/198_tips_small_lots.htm~mainFrame
http://www.chicagobotanic.org/plantinfo/tips/small_space_gardening

Along with pleasant gardens, there are other products and services that assist with relaxation and stress reduction.

Relaxation Aids:
http://www.abundanthealth4u.com/Relaxation_Ideas_s/214.htm
http://www.hgtv.com/design/rooms/bathrooms/the-relaxing-benefits-of-at-home-saunas
http://bestsauna.reviews/

http://naha.org/
https://www.verywell.com/aromatherapy-massage-89736

The above links and the following endnotes were active at the time of the publication of this book. I encourage you to continue your own research in these categories.

End Notes

[1] **Luddite Fallacy:** http://www.economicshelp.org/blog/6717/economics/the-luddite-fallacy/

[2] **AI Concerns:** http://www.mirror.co.uk/news/uk-news/rise-machines-pentagon-chiefs-say-8772439
https://www.quantamagazine.org/20150421-concerns-of-an-artificial-intelligence-pioneer/

[3] **Future is rosy:** https://thereisonlyr.com/our-inevitable-future-9d3bd616f764#.8vjb8uojh

[4] **Stress:** http://www.apa.org/monitor/2011/01/stressed-america.aspx

[5] **Transportation:** http://hosted.ap.org/dynamic/stories/U/US_LYFT_AUTONOMOUS_CARS?SITE=AP&SECTION=HOME&TEMPLATE=DEFAULT&CTIME=2016-09-18-18-45-06

[6] **Robots and jobs:** http://www.bbc.com/news/technology-33327659

[7] **Singularity:** http://content.time.com/time/magazine/article/0,9171,2048299,00.html

[8] **Advertising methods:** http://managementhelp.org/marketing/advertising/methods.htm

[9] **Food preparation safety:** http://www.fsis.usda.gov/wps/portal/fsis/topics/food-safety-education/get-answers/food-safety-fact-sheets/meat-preparation

[10] **Smartphone options:** https://www.cnet.com/news/can-you-ditch-your-smartphone-data-plan-for-wi-fi/

From the Author

I hope you have enjoyed the information presented in this book and come away with ideas for utilizing some Selective Luddite principles.

I had been unknowingly practicing Selective Luddism starting sometime in 2005 and have been moving more and more to a minimalist life since my initial downsizing started. Many of the points contained in this book are the result of this journey and my research has turned up additional valuable recommendations. My current lifestyle precludes me from trying all of the creative downsizing ideas that others are practicing. I really would like to hit the road in an RV, for instance, something I have never done. But maybe someday - who knows?

If you have Millennials in your family, or friends that have Millennials, I highly recommend my book that was mentioned earlier, 'Clueless 101, A Life Manual for Millennials'. This is a 125-page book that is full of life advice and tips for young people. You can find it on Amazon with my other books.

Best Regards,

J. Ronald Adair   www.embracingluddism.com

Other books by the author:

'Clueless 101, A Life Manual for Millennials'

'Killer 42, It's Not Your Daddy's Dominos'

'The Master Artists Adult Coloring Book I-IV'

CPSIA information can be obtained
at www.ICGtesting.com
Printed in the USA
FFOW01n1004170117
31439FF